Top Agent

"If you do what you've always done, you'll get what you've always gotten."

–**Tony Robbins**

Top Agent

Stories of Success from Industry-Leading Real Estate Professionals

Volume Five

Keith Dougherty

XMS

Florida

Top Agent

Copyright © 2017 Keith Dougherty

All rights reserved.

XMS Publishing

1391 NW St. Lucie West Blvd, Suite 247

Port St. Lucie, FL 34986

xmspublishing.com

This publication is designed to provide accurate and authoritative information regarding the subject matter covered. It is sold with the understanding that the publisher is not engaged in rendering legal, accounting, medical, or other professional services.

The information and opinions presented in this book are intended for educational purposes only. Any income claims or results discussed in this book are not typical and they are for example only.

ISBN-10: 0692964029

ISBN-13: 978-0692964026

Published in the United States of America

"Limitations live only in our minds. But if we use our imaginations, our possibilities become limitless." –Jamie Paolinetti

Dedication

This book is dedicated to every child out there that is fighting a life-threatening illness. Our thoughts and prayers are with you every day. Never give up and always keep fighting.

Table of Contents

Introduction

Welcome to Top Agent. One day, I had a notion. I said to myself, "Why don't you host your own radio show." Little did I know that I would focus solely on successful people in real estate. My show first started on Business Innovators Magazine and has now grown to Real Estate Innovators Radio (http://realestateinnovatorsradio.com/). If you are an agent reading this and you want to be considered for the show, just go to our site and submit a request to be interviewed. Please be patient, as our guest list has grown significantly.

Okay, now back to my story of how this book came to life. I was interviewing and meeting great people, many of whom you will meet in this book. They are top agents, brokers, and business owners. But the most important thing is that they are real people, no matter how much success they had. The common trait you will see they all share is that they truly care about other people. They care about finding out what people need and helping people fill that need.

So, after my 19th show, I said to myself, "You need to share these stories of success with everyone." And so, Top Agent was born.

Now, to make it even better, all the contributors to this book and I have decided to donate 100% of the retail royalties to charity, specifically St. Jude Children's Research Hospital. Per their website, "St. Jude is leading the way the world understands, treats and defeats childhood cancer and other life-threatening diseases."

If you would like to donate and support this great charity to help kids, you can visit: stjude.org.

Top Agent Samantha Walker

Samantha Walker is with Capstone Realty based out of Huntsville, Alabama. She has been selling real estate for five years, as of September first, this year and has recently been awarded the cover of Top Agent Magazine, with her success story featured inside.

Also, she received an award through Expert Network, as top three percent in the nation, with her bio and press release published. She has also provided for Top Agent Magazine, an article.

She has also been selected as a Pinnacle Professional and inducted as a member into the continental who's who and recognized for her outstanding leadership and achievements in her industry and profession. Her bio is expanded on Google.

What led you into real estate? Was it something you always knew you wanted to do? Or did you maybe stumble into it?

It's something I've always wanted to do, ever since high school. I had a family member who was a realtor and I saw her flexibility, I saw the time that she was able to spend with her family, also while being productive as one of the top agents in the Northwest Alabama area.

As I graduated high school, I ended up going to college and working in Missile Defense. I have wanted to sell Real Estate for 17 years and I thought, well if I don't just jump into it if I don't do it now, I'm never going to do it. I just have to jump and take my leap of faith.

I quit my full-time job in Missile Defense, and jumped into real estate, sold my first house in two weeks and have been selling full-time ever since four years this past September. I used to watch the home shows all the time when I was a little girl growing up. I was always fascinated with the different styles, different types of homes. This has really become my dream career. I know that I am doing what I was meant to do.

What personal attributes, traits or qualities you think have most contributed to the success that you've had in real estate?

I had a bad experience before I ever activated my license with realtors trying to sell my home and not receiving the best communication possible, coming to the closing table, and bringing a lot of money out of pocket. When I jumped into this business was, I asked myself, what's going to set me apart from other professionals? What's going to differentiate me from other Realtors? And that is my communication. I feel like I have a really driven personality and set high goals and expectations for myself to surpass and exceed. I'm always creating new, innovative ideas to offer my clients to allow them the best marketing in being the most marketable and to sell as quickly as possible, also while making them the most return on their investment. I would say my number one strength is my communication. As for buyers, I ensure they are getting the best deals and not paying more than a home is worth.

Do you think you could give an example of when these traits have put a roll in your path towards success?

As I mentioned before, this just isn't a job to me. I feel like my success is accomplished due to my availability, always being available when my clients need me and offering them the best customer service as I possibly can. I work seven days a week, nights and weekends as needed, and even while on vacation.

I was on a cruise not too long ago, and my phone stayed on. I had about five closings that week, I had listings that I had to put in the system. I just told my husband, "My job never stops, if my clients need me I want them to be able to reach me at all times." So, that goes back to my communication, and my availability to them.

A realtor's job is not a Monday through Friday, 8 to 5. If you want to be successful, you must put in the time, you should put in the hours, and be very dedicated in this business.

Can you talk a little bit about some of the obstacles and trials that you've had to overcome, in order to achieve your goals?

In the beginning of a new realtors' career, you wake up unemployed. You don't work, you don't eat. I began cold-calling to get myself started. The very first day, I jumped into the business and activated my license. I drove around and wrote 20 For-Sale-By-Owner's phone numbers on a yellow pad. I went home and I called every single phone number. You may get 20 people telling you no before you finally get a yes. But I didn't stop calling and I would call every day, all day until I built a referral based business, and then I didn't have that much time to call anymore. Listings are where the business is at because, without listings, buyers wouldn't exist.

With listings, you get referrals, you get buyers. I went from having zero listings to having 10 in my first month of being a new agent. I ended up listing 60 within my first six months.

Why didn't you give up? What was your driving force?

As I mentioned previously, being a new realtor, if you don't work, you don't eat. We don't make any money if we don't sell anything. I have that driven mindset that kept me going. That plays into my mind of being unstoppable until I exceed and surpass my goals.

What's your vision for your business and your career over the next five years?

I am very inspired to teach and train others about what I've learned, and how to overcome rejection and objections in this career. I could see myself giving back and offering my knowledge by possibly getting my Instructors License and becoming a trainer. I think that would be something I would enjoy.

What do you feel is the best way you market yourself, as a real estate professional, so you can have continual growth?

My goal is to strive to exceed my clients' expectations, to give them my best always so they can pass my name to friends and family and speak about their satisfaction with my services. In my opinion, when you provide the best service possible to clients, you are marketing yourself, which will lead to more referrals.

What do you think the biggest misconception or myth people have about working with a real estate agent?

I feel like a lot of us are viewed as being pushy. Just that next typical salesman out for money only and out for themselves. I won't deny that I feel like some are, but a good realtor, in my opinion, will be empathetic and sympathize with their client's needs, striving to find them their perfect home. And, for a seller, sell their home as quickly as possible. It's like driving through a car lot. You just don't want to be noticed. You want to look at cars but the minute that salesman walks out the door you're trying to take off and run.

What advice would you give them about selecting an agent that could best serve their needs?

Research, research, research. I always suggest interviewing more than one agent because everyone has different ideas about how they market themselves, or how they're going to market their home. Read testimonies and reviews about the realtors that you find. A lot of people may not have any out there, but make sure that they are a full-time agent. That's really important.

I hear a lot of sellers say, "You know, I never heard from my agent but they did have a full-time job." You need to make sure that you are number one priority when you're trying to sell your home.

Check to see how many listings an agent has. Sometimes they may only have a few or none. Which, to me, that demonstrates that they are new or that they don't generate a lot of business. Because the more listings you have, the more likely you are to find a buyer for that particular home.

I've sold over 19 of my own homes in the last several months because of the advertising that I provide. I'm carrying about 30-40 listings right now in my inventory. I may have a buyer call about one home in a price range that they're looking for but can possibly offer the same inventory in another area they may be looking in.

I also suggest asking an agent how much they pay towards advertising because, in order to make money, we have to spend money. Those agents that don't pay much towards their advertising tells me that they're just an agent that only puts it in MLS and leaves it, hoping someone will find it, or another realtor will just come in and sell it. Like I said, the more money you spend the more you're going to sell.

What's the best way they can find out more information about you and how you can help them?

I have my personal web page which is samanthawalkerrealestate.com. You can also find me on Zillow.com, search for Samantha Walker, and you can read my reviews and testimonials and see my inventory. I use a professional photographer so feel free to look at my listings and see some of the work that he does for me.

I was recently awarded top three percent in the nation with Expert Network, so you can find me on Google and read my WordPress article and my biography. I was on the cover of Top Agent Magazine for the state of Alabama with my success story featured inside which can also be found online.

Also, recently in the works, I received an award for Continental Who's Who, in alliance with Forbes Magazine. That was really exciting. Those are a few of the places that you can go read and learn more about me.

Top Agent Judi Wright

Judi Wright, of the Judi Wright Team of Ebby Halliday Realtors, is based out of Frisco, Texas. For 14 years, Judi Wright has been helping residential buyers and sellers in the North Texas market achieve their real estate goals. Although she has earned countless awards including D Magazines Best Realtor in Dallas title ten times, Judi measures her success on the quality of her relationships rather than the quantity of her transactions. With over 95% of her business coming from referrals, it's obvious her clients agree she is the top realtor in their books also. A certified luxury homes specialist and certified negotiation expert, Judi combines her vast experience and skills with unwavering tenacity to guide each and every client through the process to achieve the best possible outcome for them.

What led you to real estate? Was it something that you always knew that you wanted to do?

I stumbled into it actually. I started taking classes in between corporate jobs thinking that it was something I would get my license for when I retired in the future, and I liked it so much I decided I wanted to try it, and so I did.

What personal attributes, traits or qualities have most contributed to your success and how did you develop these?

I've always had a really strong work ethic in my previous corporate career, with sales and marketing, and some of those skills and easily translated over to real estate. When you're selling a home, you're marketing it. Just like when you market a product, you're packaging it and presenting it to the market in the best possible manner to try to maximize the value. I think like those skills crossed over and made it easier for me. I'm a natural connector/networker and kind of socially active person, and those skills have also crossed over and contributed to my success, I think. When you're moving people to a new area, being able to connect them with hairdressers, doctors, dentists, grocery stores, just anything and everything that people who are moving or new people moving into a new area need, I feel like having those natural skills have served me well.

Can you give a specific example of when these traits have played a role in your path towards success?

I've had people move to the area and be very scared. They never moved before, they don't know anybody, and I've connected them with a daycare for their children and helped them find a neighborhood that's exactly what they were looking for maybe with community amenities, but it's something that they were interested in. I've connected people where I helped a spouse find a job in the area through my connections and my network of clients and friends, and I've helped people find doctors, dentists, hairdressers, just about anything and everything. You'd be amazed, I regularly get texts from clients that I've helped about five years ago, "We need to replace a window. Who do you know?" I mean, it's a continual thing, it doesn't end. The relationship doesn't end when you purchase the home. I just kind of become a lifelong resource to them and I think that that helps when you're new to an area specifically.

What were some of the major adversities and trials that you had to overcome to achieve your goals?

When I first went into real estate as a single mother of two boys, not receiving child support at that point in time, and it was very scary so I had to borrow money from my 401-K to get started to fund my business, and I think doing that really fueled my passion for working. I mean, you work harder because I knew I had to. I didn't have a choice. I had kids to feed and one of them was a couple of years in college so I was responsible for getting them to college. My obstacles were more about becoming self-employed, insuring myself, feeding my children, getting my business started, and then learning how to run it successfully.

It's a whole different thing when you're self-employed, all the different systems and things you have to put into place and all the different things I had to do. The first year was hard, but it was so fun. I liked it so much that it didn't feel hard. Looking back on it now, I know how hard it was, but I was very fortunate to sell a house on my first week in the business, so I guess it wasn't as bad as it could have been is what I'm saying, but I definitely had to overcome being afraid of failure.

What kept you going despite these obstacles? Why didn't you give up?

Well, I've always believed in hard work and as I said, I was having so much fun doing it. I got a lot of fulfillment out of helping buyers and sellers accomplish their goals and sometimes their dreams. With first time home buyers, it was really exciting to me every time I put a first-time home buyer in a home because I could still remember when I bought my first home. I think I got a lot of enjoyment out of helping people and I knew that my hard work would set an example for my boys. It's so important to me that they understand that hard work can pay off. I got a lot of enjoyment and I was able to set an example for them later on and send them to college debt free so I didn't give up because it was very enjoyable, I guess would be the best thing to say.

What is your vision for your career for the next five years?

I just became a team this year on January 1st, so that's pretty new for me. I added three additional agents and a transaction coordinator to my team, so we went from one assistant and one agent to four agents and an assistant and a transaction coordinator, so that was pretty big and new this year. So, my goal, I think I just want to double our business in five years, probably have three more agents, maybe a marketing specialist and a listing specialist on staff. But I would only want to do that if we can continue to offer the same level of service and personal support to our buyers and sellers because honestly for me, the size of the business is the less important thing, happy customers are.

What do you feel is the best way you market yourself as a real estate professional for continual growth?

I think it's really important that our clients see our personality and know that we are here to help every step of the way. Our team is very personable, approachable and very available. You won't find them as a general voicemail at night that says, "If you're calling after 6 p.m., then we'll call you back tomorrow." We don't do that. We answer our phones, and real estate is a people business, but it's filled with legal and negotiation challenges and I think it is really important that our clients feel like someone is available to help them every step of the way because people get scared in real estate, and there are lots of scary little things. We try to take the fear out of the process for them. We want to reduce the stress to as little as possible, and we can't stay awake 24 hours a day, but we want our clients to feel like we're always there for them, and I think it's working for us. About 95% of our business comes from repeat customers or referral from repeat customers and that's really how we grow our business every year, so I think that's apparently important to our clients also.

What's the biggest misconception/myth people have about working with a real estate agent?

I think the misconception is that a lot of people think we showed you three houses, we write the contract and we make a bunch of money and they don't see the myriad of details that we attend to every day related to a contract for the purchase or sale of a home.

An example, I have a seller recently here in Texas who's a lawyer and Texas allows them to sell his own home. He doesn't have to use a realtor and he actually wanted to do it himself. He thought he could do it easily and save a lot of money. He thought to pay a realtor was a waste of money, and very quickly into the process, he had his home on the market. He was doing open houses and going about the process of selling it and, I don't know, but three or four weeks later I got a phone call from him and he said, "Come to my house and list my home." So, I came here expecting to give him my whole marketing presentation and show him everything I could do and he said, "No, I want your listing agreement. I'm signing it right now."

After three weeks of trying to handle it himself, he said he never wanted to deal with it again, and we sold his home in eight days and successfully closed it in less than 30. He's a very happy seller. We deal with all of the things for you; from making sure earnest money and option money gets delivered on time, the title commitment and HOA docs are delivered, and making sure that we meet all the contract provisions, negotiating the repairs, dealing with appraisers, and sometimes even helping the sell the client's furniture, we do it all.

We're reminding people that utilities need to be turned on and off. We're making sure repair receipts are correct and we're providing all the things that people need and probably one of the biggest things we're doing is that we're keeping clients out of legal problems.

When receiving a contract there are many times that people don't understand exactly what they need to do so we're navigating them through that process and sometimes we're just there to listen, but we do it all from one end to the other and sometimes I look at my email folders of my clients. I look at them. There are 1500 emails related to a 3-week closing on a property, and that doesn't count the phone calls. It's amazing how much time and effort can go into it and I think that no one sees the behind-the-scenes work that we do.

If you were to get a call from a family member in another state, wanting to sell their home, what advice would you give them about selecting an agent that can best serve their needs?

I think it's really important when people are picking an agent, to make sure that they are picking an agent that does more than just put a sign in the yard. They need to pick someone who has a strong marketing, both digital and print, someone who makes sure and hires a professional photographer. They do high-quality brochures. I think that there are all kinds of realtors out there with all different personalities and there are all different levels of marketing and marketing plans, and that of course, every market itself is different, but even in a healthy market, which we're lucky to be in right here in Frisco, Texas, even in a healthy market, marketing of a property makes a difference in how many offers you get and in the eventual price you get. I see it every day at how fast our properties get offers and how much better we do as a percentage of our offers. So, I think someone who has great marketing plans, digital and print, and then take a look at their years of experience, and particularly, their experience in negotiating.

There are a lot of agents that reduce commissions and do all types of things like that, and I don't like it. If they're willing to just reduce their commissions right off the top, they're either probably also not going to negotiate really hard for you in selling your home or buying your home.

So those are skill sets that I think are really important and it's pretty easy to search through and see if someone has that marketing plan and then talking to them, you can see what type of negotiation skill they have.

How can someone that needs a real estate agent find out more about you and how you can help?

They can visit my website, www.judiwright.com. They can see lots of information there about me and the real estate market. They can read my blog. They can find out about me and my team, and they can also call me at 214-597-2985. We are here to help and we care

Top Agent Anthony Marguleas

Anthony Marguleas, of Amalfi Estates based out of Pacific Palisades, California has owned his own philanthropic real estate firm, Amalfi Estates, for 22 years and has personally sold close to $1 billion in properties. Most recently, he was honored to be selected by the Wall Street Journal as one of the top 60 agents in the country out of one million agents. He is most proud that his team gives 10% of their net commissions to local charities with their goal of giving away $1 million.

What led you to real estate? Was it something that you always knew that you wanted to do?

Well, out of college, I started a real estate development company and I had that for a few years and then I started a real estate mortgage company in 1993 and had that for about 15 years, and then in 1994 I started my residential brokerage firm, Amalfi Estates, and I have that still today.

What personal attributes, traits or qualities have most contributed to your success and how did you develop these?

About 25 years ago, I was diagnosed with a rare type of cancer, rhabdomyosarcoma and it was Stage 4. I ended up having a bone marrow transplant and luckily everything went well. This caused me to be very grateful and appreciative every day and to not get too worried or stressed out when an obstacle or a transaction gets in my way. We just put everything into perspective and we're very optimistic about how we handle any challenges that come along.

What were some of the major adversities and trials that you had to overcome to achieve your goals?

They all pale in comparison to having a life-threatening disease, but we've had situations where, whether it's a seller or the buyer or other agents involved, that can be a little challenging. I've had my company for 22 years and we've helped over 600 families buy and sell homes, so we've come across several different situations, where not everyone has been the easiest to work with, and one thing that we've done, we've just been very patient and we're very creative in putting the deal together. The fun part of our job is making complex deals happen and thinking outside of the box.

What kept you going despite these obstacles? Why didn't you give up?

I have a lot of energy and I like challenges, and I don't believe in giving up. A lot of what we do, we're here to make a difference. Our company is a philanthropic real estate brokerage firm and we give 10% of our net commission back to the community and back to local charities and it's made a very impactful difference in not only our lives but more importantly our clients' lives as well as the community. It also helped the Sales Partners I have on my team to solidify the philosophy of giving back. Once we started it, we knew it was the right thing to do.

What is your vision for your career for the next five years?

My goal is to give $1 million to charity. We are currently giving about $150,000 a year, and we've selected five local charities; for kids, Make-A-Wish, for pets, SPCALA, Health, American Cancer Society, Homelessness and a local one Homeboy Industries that helps people get out of gangs. I am very excited to give a million dollars back to these amazing 5 charities, and we're almost halfway there now. My real goal is that we can help influence other agents throughout the country to give 10% back as well. So, it won't just be me giving a million dollars, it will be a $100 million or $200 million going to charities all over the country, as that would be truly exciting. That is my vision.

What do you feel is the best way you market yourself as a real estate professional for continual growth?

We've been very fortunate to have grown our sales every year, and the longer we're in the business, the more referrals we get. We advertise heavily, both in print and online, and we do a lot of social media, and our charitable giving also gets coverage. People really resonate, with our commitment to the community. It really deepens our relationship with our client and we believe it honors that relationship with that charitable donation.

What's the biggest misconception/myth people have about working with a real estate agent?

I think the biggest misconception or myth is not understanding the value that a good agent can bring to the table. I think the barrier to entry for our industry is very low at least in California. When I started, it only took about 20 hours to get a real estate license, and it was ranked as one of the lowest professions, and a lot of it had to do with how easy it was to get a license.

Having a good agent who's got a long track record, and has taken extensive negotiating classes is very important. I've been fortunate to be a guest lecturer at UCLA for their real estate class the past 14 years. I've also published 300 real estate articles and written a couple of books on real estate, so the value that a good agent can bring is invaluable. The misconception or myth that people have is lumping all agents together when there are many agents that are very, very good at what they do.

If you were to get a call from a family member in another state, wanting to sell their home, what advice would you give them about selecting an agent that can best serve their needs?

I would make sure to check their references. Yelp is a great avenue for objectively checking references. I know several online sites like Zillow and Realtor.com are great references as well. I'd also check how much experience they have selling homes in that specific area as well at that specific price range. A lot of times someone will pick a friend or family member or maybe someone a friend or family member referred. However, the reality is they may not be a specialist in that exact area or in that price range.

How can someone that needs a real estate agent find out more about you and how you can help?

We specialize in selling homes in Pacific Palisades, Brentwood, Santa Monica, Beverly Hills and in the Malibu areas. Our website is AmalfiEstates.com like the Amalfi Coast in Italy, and my cell phone is 310-293-9280.

Top Agent Desmond Milvenan

Desmond Milvenan, of Engel & Völkers Austin, is based out of Austin, Texas. With over 15 years' tenure in Austin real estate, Desmond has experienced many of the various market cycles. Her involvement in the banking industry during boom and bust gives her an edge in navigating housing markets. She was recently named a Private Office Advisor at Engel & Völkers and was the Top Producer for 2015 for the Austin shop location. She further distinguished herself by earning a membership multiple times in Elite 25 (Elite 25® represents Austin real estate agents that are top 1% in the high-end real estate market). She was inducted into the Platinum Top 50 Realtors and is a member of Who's Who in Luxury Real Estate and the Board of Regents.

She was rated by the Austin Business Journal as one of the Top 25 Austin Realtors for 2015. An expert in her field, she has earned multiple designations including Certified Luxury Home Marketing Specialist, Certified Residential Specialist – an honor bestowed upon only to 4% of agents – in Graduate Realtor Institute, and her newest is Resort & Second-Home Property Specialist. In addition to her passion for real estate, she is involved with the American Heart Association Go Red for Women campaign in spreading the word about women's health.

Although she specializes in marketing and selling luxury real estate, no job is too large or too small – she devotes personal attention to each client and individual situation and consistently finds the best possible outcomes for her clients.

What led you to real estate? Was it something that you always knew that you wanted to do?

I worked in banking for many years handling asset management. A lot of that time was during the downturn, so I dealt with foreclosures, bank closures, and all kinds of other not so positive things. After banking, I stayed at home with my very young children for a couple of years but knew I wanted to go back to work. Even before I actually got in real estate my husband encouraged me to look into it. I had a friend who had a pretty large real estate team, and she said, "How do you like to come be my director of first impression?" And I said, "Well, what's that?" She said, "Reception in her real estate office." I thought, "Well, that's a good way to get my feet wet after being out of the market for a couple of years." After Day 1, I knew I could do well in real estate and so I immediately went and got my license.

What personal attributes, traits or qualities have most contributed to your success and how did you develop these?

A lot of what I learned in banking really did help me in my business. Over the years, as many of us have done, I have taken a number of personality tests and they consistently indicated that I'm pretty determined and social. When I thought about it, "Okay, what kind of career would be a good match for both of those traits?" Real estate seemed to be a natural fit.

Can you give a specific example of when these traits have played a role in your path towards success?

Yes, I'm pretty goal oriented and there was one transaction, in particular, that was one of those situations where people kept saying, "Just let it go. It's a lost cause, just let it go.", including my broker at the time. My clients had a home that they really needed to sell. They were having some financial difficulties, and they had a first and second lien on the property. They were going through the foreclosure process, and if you've ever worked in that market you know, it's tough enough when you're working with one lienholder, much less two. This was a very, very tricky short sale to workout. There was so much back and forth and back and forth leading up to everyone kind of saying, "You can't do it. It won't get done." Well, I got it done and we sold the house. My clients didn't have a foreclosure on their background and could move forward in a new home.

What were some of the major adversities and trials that you had to overcome to achieve your goals?

It's hard to hear rejection of any kind but when you're in sales you have to learn to let it roll off your back and look to the next day and start all over. I had to just learn not to become negative about rejections, and luckily, there wasn't that many of them. I always try to remember, "Every day is a new day and we're going to start at the top and not worry about those deals that you didn't get."

My children have all grown up but at the time I had three young children who were involved in sports and extracurricular activities and so often my timing is my clients' timing. It wasn't always the most convenient for us as a family and that gets a little tricky. My husband also has a very challenging career which makes for a lot of work-life balancing. Luckily, he is so supportive and between the two of us, we always manage to be where we need to be for the kids and my career.

What kept you going despite these obstacles? Why didn't you give up?

I'm really competitive. You start out, "Well, this is my goal for the quarter or this is my goal for the year," and then it becomes, "I want to be part of this organization or I want to qualify for this distinction." It quickly got to be, "I want to be the top producer for my company and for my brand." I think I was just too competitive to quit.

I enjoy helping others and real estate has been a great opportunity to make a career out of it. In fact, I used to be a matchmaker in high school and college. I love putting people together and that has kind of have morphed into matching sellers with buyers.

What is your vision for your career for the next five years?

I love to teach other people, help them grow, learn and succeed. There is plenty of business for everybody and I always try to encourage other agents. One of my goals is to start taking on more of a management and mentoring role with other agents that are learning. I'm thinking about managing my own team and taking more buyer and seller agents under my wing.

What do you feel is the best way you market yourself as a real estate professional for continual growth?

I tell new agents this all the time, "Get out in the community, meet people constantly. Don't be afraid to say you're in real estate. Don't be afraid to ask for the business. Don't be afraid to give out your cards." Also, I know a lot of people don't do this but I think print ads, consistent print ads, in your community are a great thing. People start to automatically associate me with the real estate business. When they see me, they'll come up and ask a real estate question, not that they're necessarily going to buy or sell. They might just want to know about their mortgage. You want to be known as that expert. Meeting people and having them see your name in print is one of the best ways to do that.

What's the biggest misconception/myth people have about working with a real estate agent?

Well, it's funny because if you look at how realtors are rated in the food chain of jobs, we're way, way down at the bottom. I kind of think people view us as little lower than a used car salesmen. Which is really not true. There are so many realtors that are so professional, smart and committed to their clients. When you work with an agent, their goal is to help you find the best house with the best price and something that at the end of the day makes you say, "I'm so happy with this sale or with this buy." I think in this market when there are so many other factors, people will be remiss not to use a realtor.

If you were to get a call from a family member in another state, wanting to sell their home, what advice would you give them about selecting an agent that can best serve their needs?

I tell people to go ahead and interview several agents, and when you're interviewing them, ask them, "What is your marketing plan?" If they look like a deer in the headlights, they're probably not the right agent for you. I would also advise them to ask, "What are your suggestions for getting my property ready to sell? What price should we list at?" Does the agent have a plan for communicating with you? Do you think that you can work as a team in getting your house sold? The most important thing is to find an agent you're comfortable with.

How can someone that needs a real estate agent find out more about you and how you can help?

They can call, text, email, look on the website, a number of different ways. My phone number is 512-294-4740. My email is desmondm@kw.com.

Top Agent Jay Heckendorn

In 1989, Jay Heckendorn-Telenda, of Keller Williams Realty based out of Orlando, Florida, entered the real estate industry at the ripe age of 18 with the mission of "Outstanding relationships attract new raving fans every day," setting out his belief that "it's all about relationships." In light of the collapsing Southern California market, he directed his energies towards assisting new home builders in closing out their standing inventory by means of equity trades, bulk sales, and traditional marketing methods. He successfully formed and managed several mortgage-backed investment funds via private offerings, and he has managed the disposition and sale of over 7,500 residential properties nationwide and is well versed in foreclosure, bankruptcy, loss mitigation and workouts, trends and processes.

Jay also brings a strong background in valuation, renovation and disposition methods, and techniques. In 2010, he proudly joined the esteemed team of high caliber agents at Keller Williams Classic in Orlando, Florida as Director of REO & Workouts. He consistently ranks on the Top 250 agents nationwide (top .0001%) by Wall Street Journal and Realtrends, and according to the Orlando Regional Realtor Association, he closed more sales than any other agent in Central Florida last year, and according to Keller Williams, he is #1 for closed transactions in the entire southeast region.

What led you to real estate? Was it something that you always knew that you wanted to do?

As a child, I helped my mother clean model homes at new construction sites at night and I was always curious about seeing the different layouts and designs of the homes, but it's actually affordability and plans that's got interesting the most. So, what I would do is I'll look at the price sheet, I'd figure out what the payments would be, how much they would have to earn in order to purchase the homes and I just have a curiosity that way.

But that said though, well, it was actually my first love and ambition, and however, I moved out on my own at a young age and I've had strong earnings as a sales manager for Singer Sewing Machine Company, but unfortunately, I did not qualify for financial aid to go to college and that led me to thinking "what else can I do" that I thought about families such as Getty and Rockefeller and Kennedy and such, and while they all have their businesses in various industries, the amassed their wealth in real estate, and so there's no sense of me reinventing the wheel and so real estate it was.

What personal attributes, traits or qualities have most contributed to your success and how did you develop these?

My values are trustworthiness, achievement, and fun, and so I define trustworthiness as both character and confidence, achievement is given, and of course, if you're going to do stuff and at that point doing it. Throughout my career, my mission statement has always been outstanding, relationships, attracting new raving fans every day. I've been principle and relationship-based. Rather than focusing on sales admission, I focus on the relationship and the sales always follow.

Can you give a specific example of when these traits have played a role in your path towards success?

In the beginning, when I built the general residential business, 75% of the business came from referrals from past clients or my sphere of influence. However, relationships that I had with various banks opened the door for me to begin purchasing scores of non-performing mortgages, securitize mortgages, and then service them as I work them out and sold the loans off.

A few years later, another bank gave me an opportunity to manage their contractors and brokers in marketing and sales with their foreclosures along the East Coast, so both of these ventures came from the trades and relationships that were developed and they were very successful ones that catapulted me to higher levels.

What were some of the major adversities and trials that you had to overcome to achieve your goals?

I began when I was 18, baby-faced young man in Los Angeles, and so initially it was quite challenging to earn the trust of clients and have them take me seriously. However, I came that. I used knowledge to compensate for my usefulness, so I took a lot of additional courses and finance and real estate law and title, and then also I had a couple of amazing mentors that took interest and took me under their wings. I absorbed everything I could from them and applied it and their insight and guidance were invaluable, so they always gave me ideas that were outside of the box and helped me connect the dots that way, but that was definitely key in helping me rise above the age barrier that I faced.

What kept you going despite these obstacles? Why didn't you give up?

Well, to be frank, I lived on my own and I provided for my grandmother so there really wasn't an option and I did not view any obstacles as something that cannot be overcome so you just press forward and make it work.

What is your vision for your career for the next five years?

At the moment, I'm repositioning focus back to the retail market and building a team of very gifted and talented agents that would capture a greater share of the growing market as our economy has recovered. However, when the next recession hit, they'll shift back to the mortgage follow-up industry to capture both the sales and the foreclosures, but I'll also set up two different funds, one to purchase non-performing mortgages and one to purchase foreclosed real estate to hold as rentals and that will also trickle down and pay for the team to piggyback going during the next recession.

What do you feel is the best way you market yourself as a real estate professional for continual growth?

I'd say be different. I choose an edge and I focus on the needs of the clients in that market versus the typical ego-driven marketing that's prevalent. Also, be involved in the community so schools, charities, boys and girls club or YMCA or any other civic organizations, and then finally, I'd look for problems, whether it's within my duties in serving in charities and boys and girls club. I look for problems or issues that may be trending in the marketplace and then I work to bring solutions for that.

What's the biggest misconception/myth people have about working with a real estate agent?

That's a great question. I would say that's exactly the misconception is that agents cost money. The reality is that a good or seasoned agent is most likely to fetch a higher price for their clients they're selling or negotiate a lower price for their buying client. There are also liabilities that come with real estate so I have a saying if you think hiring an experienced agent is expensive, go ahead and see an inexperienced agent.

If you were to get a call from a family member in another state, wanting to sell their home, what advice would you give them about selecting an agent that can best serve their needs?

I would suggest first searching the internet for the real trends, top 250, who are the top 250 agents out of 1.6 million in the United States, and I would look to see if there's an agent on that list that services their area. Agents at that level, they have the greatest experience through their high number of transactions, and obviously, with each transaction, it's another experience, and they also have the infrastructure and the systems in place to provide the highest level of service.

However, if there are no top 250 agents servicing that area, then I would ask friends. I would also call a few title or escrow companies to find out what agents they're doing most of the business in the area, and then I would think it's a good idea when interviewing agents to ask the agent who they believe their strongest competitors are, and then that expands that out.

How can someone that needs a real estate agent find out more about you and how you can help?

We have a website, it's www.yourorlandorealestate.com, and then my telephone number is area code 214-244-7857.

Top Agent Julie Wyss

Julie Wyss, of Keller Williams Bay Area Estates based out of Los Gatos, California, has been in real estate for eight years full time with a broker's license. Her husband joined the team two years ago, and they have focused on buyers. Her daughter serves as their full-time executive assistant and project manager.

Julie's awards and recognitions include Rookie of the Year 1st year in real estate, top individual agent and top 1% of company (Intero Los Gatos – 2013), #3 individual agent of the entire company (Keller Williams – 2015), Wall Street Real Trends (#244 in 2015), and real estate agent Bay Area #50 out of 100 in 2015 for the Leading 100.

What led you to real estate? Was it something that you always knew that you wanted to do?

I'd say it was more of a natural progression. It wasn't something that I knew I always wanted to do. I was a mortgage broker for a period of time and when the market changed in '07, it was kind of a natural transition. Also, that was about the time my youngest child was entering into first grade, so I looked at it as a great opportunity to enter a full-time career in real estate, and a couple of other things such as the unlimited income potential as well as a flexible schedule was very attractive.

What personal attributes, traits or qualities have most contributed to your success and how did you develop these?

I'm very certain that it's my personal attention in relationship building, ongoing communications, so I really will be connected to my clients at all times and I know that they appreciate that. Also, with instructors or mentors that give me tips for success, I actually execute them, put them into actions. A lot of times we'll go into classes and other agents will take notes and they think about implementing it and I actually take the actions that are recommended.

Also, I would say I have exceptionally good organizational skills and I'll anticipate problems or next steps and address them rather than waiting for them to occur, so I don't put anything off, I take action immediately. I pay close attention to detail and keep the flow of information going at all times, and that way, if I'm staying ahead of the game, if something comes up or should I say when something comes up, that other agents might think that as a surprise, I am prepared because I've already taken care of everything that can be anticipated.

Additionally, I'd like to mention that I have systems in place. I'm very committed to sticking with them. So for example, working with a listing, if you're approaching it and making sure that everything has a system and on the checklist is taken care, then when new things pop up, they're easy to tackle.

Can you give a specific example of when these traits have played a role in your path towards success?

I would say with personal attention, I was a small business owner prior to being a mortgage broker and I always used to say that the best customer is the one that you already have. I'm very focused on building and maintaining these relationships. Truly caring about the person and not just the transaction, and again, another specific example is the instructor or mentor tips. I did what others told me would lead me to success. I have watched and continue to watch what high-level real estate agents are doing, and I'll make it my own and kind of do what they're doing.

I'll go back again to the systems in place. Having a system in an organization is the absolute number one key to my success. Having that in place, it allows me to be more personable with my client.

What were some of the major adversities and trials that you had to overcome to achieve your goals?

When I came into real estate, it was a short sale market and the market was considered a burst, and what I did was to just embrace it and turned it into an opportunity. Most of the agents, as I entered into real estate, were complaining and saying what a horrible time it was to be in real estate, not just short sales were. What I found was immediately at that point, if I were able to hire someone to help me take care of – at that point it was the negotiations with the banks and then later hiring assistants, transaction coordinators. Getting the help that I need is really what helped me overcome what most people would consider adverse conditions.

What kept you going despite these obstacles? Why didn't you give up?

I never considered giving up. I was committed to success. I entered the real estate market when I was older, so I've only had eight years in the business at this point, and I considered this my final career. I never considered giving up. I've always had this support of my husband, my family, and I've been building a team that supports me, and that allows me to grow the business as well.

What is your vision for your career for the next five years?

I'm planning just to charge it for the next five years. My last and youngest child has just got into high school, so I've got four more years before I could actually travel the world and I plan to just work very hard, continue doing exactly what I'm doing, continuing with the systems and then after that, gradually going to part time and allowing my husband who's also my business partner to take over a little bit more of the business.

Also, I would say that my vision for the next five years is a little bit different than most real estate agents or most high performing agents. I'm not a big fan of the team business plan. I know that that's super popular right now. I like the boutique service. I'd prefer to keep it small so I'm always going to maintain my position as the lead agent. There's outsourced help that supports me, but my clients need to know that I'm always accessible.

What do you feel is the best way you market yourself as a real estate professional for continual growth?

Online presence is the key to marketing. Weekly I scrutinize my online presence. It's on my calendar. It's something that I spend about an hour doing. I continuously update it, dial it in, and tweak it, including everything from LinkedIn, my website, Zillow, Realtor.com. I'd like to scrutinize it weekly and I also leverage all of my recognitions. So currently, on the Wall Street Journal top 1,000, I'm number 244. In the Bay Area Leading 100, I'm number 50. All of Santa Clara County, I'm number 16. I take these numbers and I leverage them and I think leveraging success is a great way to market yourself.

What's the biggest misconception/myth people have about working with a real estate agent?

I think that lots of folks think that homes sell themselves, especially when it's a seller's market, and that we're not really doing the work behind it. The misconception is all of the intricacies that go into a real estate transaction, everything from title and escrow, pricing correctly, making sure all of the disclosures are complete, helping them understand what's behind inspections when something is a red flag or something that's not a big deal, negotiating strategies. I think that the biggest misconception is that homes sell themselves and that we're simply managing the standardized contracts, and I also believe that they think that we're overcompensated to some degree, so I'd say those are some of the biggest misconceptions.

If you were to get a call from a family member in another state, wanting to sell their home, what advice would you give them about selecting an agent that can best serve their needs?

I don't necessarily refer them to somebody that's with the same agency that I'm with. I do a research. I research the market online. We search the agent's online presence. I'll do a phone interview with the agent and then I'll make the referral to the family member. I don't necessarily just refer them to someone with the same agency. A lot of times it would be based on their reviews, number of transactions. I'd like to make sure that they're in the market, that they understand the neighborhood, so I think that would be my process. Actually, I do it quite frequently.

How can someone that needs a real estate agent find out more about you and how you can help?

I can easily be located on the internet, just search my name, Julie Wyss, and of course, I'll pop up immediately. That to me is the most important and the easiest way to find me. Also, of course, my website which is just my name, julie@juliewyss.com, and you can also call me, 408-687-2026, and the great thing is, it's that I will pick up the phone, and if I don't pick up the phone, I'll call you right back.

Top Agent Sheley Bressler

Sheley Bressler, of Keller Williams Realty, is based out of Seattle, Washington. Sheley has been practicing real estate in the Greater Seattle area for 12 years. Her motto for her business is "Be Kind, Be Humble!" This motto has helped her catapult to the top of her industry in the Seattle area. She has been recognized as a 5-Star Professional for client satisfaction every year since 2010, and she was also featured on the cover story in Top Agent Magazine in January 2016.

What led you to real estate? Was it something that you always knew that you wanted to do?

It wasn't really something I knew I always wanted to do. Several years ago, in about 2003, I had a bad experience selling my own first home. The agent was not honest, he was not my advocate, and he took advantage of my inexperience. It was during that time that I became interested in becoming an agent whose focus is on education and customer service. Growing up in Seattle, I have a "Nordstrom" customer service mentality, and I wanted to bring that high-level service to real estate.

What personal attributes, traits or qualities have most contributed to your success and how did you develop these?

I come from a place of kindness and gratitude in everything I do. I realized a long time ago that if you're nice, you'll go really far in life.

Another attribute that has served me well is my creativity. I have an "idea board" at my desk where I pin up all kinds of things trying to stay creative, stay ahead of the market, what's new, and what's going to work. I think one other thing would be anticipating needs. This is a huge attribute to have as an agent. I try to stay ahead of things so that I don't have many objections to handle or fires to put out, and I also expect my team of people who support my business to have this same mentality. This helps make things go smoothly. Finally, I fail forward, meaning that when I do fail, I learn from it and I take that and put it into the next thing. I don't make excuses, and I take responsibility.

What were some of the major adversities and trials that you had to overcome to achieve your goals?

One thing that I've had to deal with is being a working mom. I have a 2-year-old son and a 5-year-old daughter, and I think that being a working mom is tough. I read a very poignant quote about a year ago, "Working moms are expected to work as though they don't have kids and parent as though they don't work." I find this to be very true. I do have a pretty good balance, especially because my husband has put his career on hold to be a stay-at-home parent. But, there's a lot of judgment out there. I need to be careful that my clients don't think I'm too busy being a mom to take excellent care of them. I think that being a mom has made me improve my systems so I'm able to serve my clients better than I ever have before.

What kept you going despite these obstacles? Why didn't you give up?

I really love what I do. I can't imagine doing anything else. As cliché as that may sound, I know I can help people, and that's a great reason to go to work every day. I also want my kids to have a strong female role model in their mother. I want both of them to know that women can do anything they put their mind to with hard work and dedication!

What is your vision for your career for the next five years?

I'm in the beginning stages of building a team. I would love to grow to a hundred transactions a year in the next five years. The most important thing here is to bring in the right people and keep implementing better and better systems to maintain the already high level of customer service that we have.

What do you feel is the best way you market yourself as a real estate professional for continual growth?

I work 100% by referral, so continuing to serve our clients and their referrals. If we keep doing that, and we keep improving on the ways that we serve them, then we should be able to reach our goals and have that continued growth.

What's the biggest misconception/myth people have about working with a real estate agent?

I think that people think that they'll make more money if they don't use an agent or use a discount brokerage. In actuality, they will make more money and have much less stress if they work with an agent like myself. My team takes care of everything for sellers, including coordinating repairs, cleaning, landscaping, home staging, and photography. And we pay for these services. We also systematized everything to easily get sellers from that moment they decide they want to sell their homes to closing escrow. On the buyer side, I can't emphasize enough how important it is to have an agent like myself educating you and advocating for you along the way. We have 100% success rate of getting buyers into a home they love!

If you were to get a call from a family member in another state, wanting to sell their home, what advice would you give them about selecting an agent that can best serve their needs?

Besides the basics of finding someone who is nice and who will answer their phone, I would like to give them seller interview questions. I give these to all sellers who are interviewing me, with the expectation that they're interviewing other agents, too. These include questions about pricing, "What goes into your pricing research and how do we develop a pricing strategy?" Or asking them, "What are your average days on market and what is your list to sale price percentage?" I think these questions can be helpful for people who are looking for an agent to help them sell their largest asset.

How can someone that needs a real estate agent find out more about you and how you can help?

A great place to start is my website, sheleybressler.com, and I can also be reached at 206-240-8740 or sheley@kw.com.

Top Agent Tracy Tran

Tracy graduated from Northern Illinois University in 1999 with a degree in Information System. She started my career at Siemens and quickly moved up the cooperate ladder to Senior Engineering. Having a passion for business I opened up a salon while still working at Siemens and taking care of 3 children. My passion for Real Estate won me over and she sold my Salon and got her Real Estate license and started selling while still working at Siemens. Siemens gave her a framework of the corporate environment and the Salon helped deal with my clients on a more personal level. Her business grew exponentially and soon I had to said goodbye to Siemens and she has never looked back since.

She has been dealt with many types of markets and had worked with distressed properties, investors, short sale, traditional sale and new construction buyers.

She is a member of International President's Elite which is leading award of Coldwell Banker and ranked #1 in her office.

What led you to real estate? Was it something that you always knew that you wanted to do?

The housing downturn hit many in my community hard with foreclosures and short sales. Many turned to me for help because of my experience in the corporate world.

I was always fascinated with Real Estate and always felt that I could do a better job than the agents in my community

What personal attributes, traits or qualities have most contributed to your success? How did you develop these?

Trust, perseverance, going that extra mile to see every transaction to the end. Sometimes I have to deal with the banks, mortgage brokers, insurance companies, inspectors, and attorney on behalf of by clients because they don't speak English.

How did I develop these?

Patience and over time.

Can you give specific examples of when these traits have played a role in your path towards success?

I deal with many short sales on behalf of my clients and these types of deals require knowledge of the process and a lot of patients. I work with a number of ethnic groups and English is not their first language. It is up to me to bridge the language barrier between them and the attorneys and mortgage companies.

What were some of the major adversities and trials that you had to overcome to achieve your goals?

One of the hardest obstacles I had was getting people to trust me at the beginning with helping then purchase or sell their largest transaction they will ever do. I was the new kid on the block and it was tough getting respect. After my first few details, word spread throughout the community on how hard I worked for my clients. Now referrals make up more than 80% of my business.

What kept you going despite these obstacles? Why didn't you give up?

People that know me well, know that I do not give up. Adversity makes me stronger. When someone tells me that I can't do it, I want to prove them wrong.

What is your vision for your career for the next five years?

I am a very driven individual and I love what I do. My goal is to open up my office and hire the best of best. Agents that are driven like me that love what they do.

What do you feel is the best way you market yourself as a real estate professional for continual growth?

Referrals are the best testament for any Real Estate Professional. When someone refers you to their friends, it means that you have done your job well and they approve of the service and guidance that you have given them along the way. I believe, service is the best way one can market themselves.

What's the biggest misconception/myth people have about working with a real estate agent?

That we are all cut from same cloth. We are not, there are good ones and then there are the bad ones. To be truly successful, you have to be willing to the interest of your clients ahead of your own.

If you were to get a call from a family member in another state, wanting to sell their home, what advice would you give them about selecting an agent that can best serve their needs?

Don't base your hiring of an agent solely on commission. A half point reduction on a 300k house is only a saving of $1500 in the end. An agent that is not a good negotiator and that is not willing to go that extra mile for you will lose you more than that in the end. An Agent that is a good negotiator can get you 5k higher with their skills.

How can someone that needs a real estate agent find out more about you and how you can help?

I am just a phone call away. I would love to meet with anyone one on one to go over their needs and budget. No two transactions are the same, each one has to be treated on its own merits.

Top Agent Ed Murchison

As a real estate professional with Virginia Cook, Realtors, Ed Murchison, based out of Dallas, Texas, serves his clients with more than 20 years of sales, marketing and project management experience and a lifetime passion for architecture and design. Ed is a realtor in the Dallas area and specializes in mid-century modern homes. He also sells architect-designed modern homes and represents several leading builders and architects in Dallas.

Ed is the exclusive listing agent for Urban Reserve which is Dallas' only green development, made up of 50 modern homes designed by over 25 different architects. He is a top producing agent at Virginia Cook, Realtors and has been recognized as a top producer by D Magazine.

What led you to real estate? Was it something that you always knew that you wanted to do?

I wouldn't use the word "stumble." It was kind of at a crossroads in my career when after 15 years in corporate America and I found out my job was moving to another state and they gave me the opportunity of either making that move or taking a nice tidy severance package, and I had already been thinking about a career change and I decided this is my opportunity to reinvent myself. So that's how I got started in real estate.

What personal attributes, traits or qualities have most contributed to your success and how did you develop these?

In particular, I love design, in particular, a good modern design in pretty much anything and everything. From architectural design to modern furniture, art, landscaping, all the way down to dinnerware, pottery, glass, you name it. I love classic cars from the 50's and 60's. I was able to apply a lot of my sales and marketing skills that I picked up as well as my business acumen from corporate America over to real estate.

I think at a time that I came into real estate, I saw a real shift in real estate occurring and I saw technology becoming more and more a backbone of the sales and marketing efforts happening in real estate. I think a lot of the agents who have been around for a really long time in the business who have done it in the old way were suddenly faced with people like me that I saw it coming into the business who have all of that experience with business world and they were bringing it in and very astutely applying it to real estate. I think those skills and experience that I gained working for a Fortune 500 company really helped me get my real estate career off to a great start.

Can you give a specific example of when these traits have played a role in your path towards success?

I think that my marketing experience was key to my success. I did a lot of marketing and marketing program designs, trade shows and all kinds of things in the corporate world and I knew as a new agent I had to figure out a way to set myself apart from the hundreds and even thousands of other agents that are out in the Dallas-Fort Worth area that had way more real estate experience than I did, and I needed to give people a reason to hire me. I knew that I had to apply what I love and what I knew too about business and how I could use that to fulfill a need in the market.

I saw this increasing interest happening in mid-century modern homes, which was something that I knew and I knew that I could take this and create a niche for myself in the market that I could build that business and serve it.

What were some of the major adversities and trials that you had to overcome to achieve your goals?

I think at the point that all of this occurred when I got into real estate, it was probably right about 40 years old and being laid off from a great corporate job and a nice salary and great benefits, it kind of left me feeling like, "Okay, am I making the right decision?" You know how hard it is because here I was starting all over in a brand new career that was going to be totally commission based, and actually it was a bit scary, but I knew deep down that I could do it, but I was going to have to work really hard at it.

I had myself been looking for a house, probably just over 20 years ago and I knew I wanted a mid-century modern house, and this was even really before that term "mid-century modern" had even been coined or was be widely used to describe this style of architecture, and what I found was that really learning no realtors out there that really understood what I was looking and what was important to me, so I ended up driving around all over the city searching out homes that I like and in the process, I became very familiar with the style and where these types of homes were located.

I think I had this in my back pocket 20-plus years ago that I had started building this and suddenly I thought, "Here's my opportunity to fulfill that niche that I saw 20 years ago that still have not been filled."

What kept you going despite these obstacles? Why didn't you give up?

For me giving up was never an option. I don't think I've ever given up on anything that I had put my mind to. I think for me, in particular, I was very lucky that I had always done a great job managing my money well and that I did not have any debt coming into the business, and this allowed me to really invest in my business and get it off to a strong start. I think many people don't realize just how expensive getting into real estate can be and how important it is that you really need to invest in your business and build that brand for yourself.

What is your vision for your career for the next five years?

Over the next five years or so, I really plan to continue to grow my business. I'd like to add some additional people to my team and my business has continued to expand to include really not only mid-century modern homes, but more and more new architect-designed modern homes. Actually, I represent Dallas' only green development, which is called Urban Reserve, which has been a really great success for me and I think it's opened up a lot of new doors. We only have a couple of properties left out of 50 in the development.

In that particular development, our developer has just purchased another tract of property and has plans underway to do kind of a more affordable version of that concept, and with the projected price point in that sweet spot between $300,000 and $500,000. We're even planning to do a few with we're terming as micro-homes that's sort of going around 650 square feet, and I think with the huge interest in tiny homes, I think there are no less than four or five different shows on the home channels focused on tiny homes.

I'm really excited to be able to offer this to the Dallas market and be kind of once again on the cutting edge of something that's really fresh and exciting to me.

What do you feel is the best way you market yourself as a real estate professional for continual growth?

For me, that market niche that I carved out for myself has really worked quite well. I really enjoy what I do and the clients that I work with, and that makes my work exciting. I think anytime you can take your business and do something that you're passionate about you're going to be successful. The clients that I work with, they tend to like and enjoy these many kinds of things that I do and many of them have become very close friends to me over the years, and I think anytime you can package the passion and be able to have that real connection with your client's successes, it's easy to achieve.

What's the biggest misconception/myth people have about working with a real estate agent?

I think what's actually in the market more and more, and I see this particularly with younger buyers, and in particular, first time home buyers, that they end up relying so heavily on the internet and there is an awful lot of information out there. The unfortunate thing about a lot of information is it's not always correct or accurate and I often find some of these buyers relying on inaccurate, incomplete information, and then finally being able to, the real estate professional, get in front of them and show them the value that you bring and that you can provide them more accurate, more timely information and that you really know the market and the neighborhoods that they're shopping and could provide that personal touch that they simply cannot get on their own looking through listings on the internet.

If you were to get a call from a family member in another state, wanting to sell their home, what advice would you give them about selecting an agent that can best serve their needs?

Fortunately, I work for a company that is part of the real estate referral network of the leading real estate companies in the world, which is really great. However, I think the most important thing for somebody like that is whoever their friends, family or whatever, I think the first thing any buyer needs to do or seller for that matter, they really need to outline what they want out of the transaction or what they want out of their next home.

Then once they got that information, they could easily communicate specifically what their needs into the INR to an agent and they can take those needs into the INR and match them up to figure out, "Is this agent a good match for me both from a knowledge level perspective as well as a personal and communicational level perspective."

How can someone that needs a real estate agent find out more about you and how you can help?

I do have my own website which attracts a lot of activity, which focuses on mid-century modern and modern homes on that website. It's midcenturymoderndallashomes.com. I'm also kind of a unique agent in that perspective that I do believe very firmly marketing is a really key component of what I do. I also do utilize really good print advertising method. There's a magazine called Atomic Ranch that has a nationwide, actually a worldwide distribution. I do advertise in that magazine because once again it funnels right into the market niche that I serve, which are mid-century modern homes. They can check out my website or check out my ad in Atomic Ranch magazine to find out more information about me.

Top Agent Debra Dobbs

Debra Dobbs, of @properties, based out of Chicago, Illinois began her real estate career 32 years ago, selling renovated loft condos in Chicago's West Loop. A Chicago Association of Realtors top 1% producer for the past 15 years, she is a Top 50 Agent in Chicago, #1 individual agent with @properties, and on the roster of Who's Who in Chicago Real Estate.

She holds multiple professional designations – the prestigious Certified Residential Specialist, Million Dollar Guild Member of the Institute for Luxury Home Marketing and graduate of the Realtor Institute, as well as an Urban Real Estate degree from the University of Illinois.

She was recently in the press for putting together a complicated deal for 12,000 square feet of residential condominiums at Water Tower on behalf of a developer client. The property had been on and off the market for many years and she represented the buyers in this transaction.

What led you to real estate? Was it something that you always knew that you wanted to do?

I definitely stumbled into real estate. It wasn't anywhere on my radar in terms of what I wanted to do when I grew up, and I actually spent a lot of time traveling around the States and Europe and opened Gelateria, produced a play, and I sort of fell into an opportunity back in 1984 and realized I loved it.

What personal attributes, traits or qualities have most contributed to your success and how did you develop these?

Patience, for certain, and that can be patient on waiting for a deal to come together. It can be patient with a first-time home buyer that needs to see 50 or 60 properties before they can make a decision, and one of my dearest friends now who started a client, his record was seeing 79 properties before she bought. My clients would describe me as a Mama Bear and they would say that I fiercely advocate for their best interest and they know that and they get that sense, and I think that's the trait that I think that I do have.

I also think it's important to know when to see the trees for the forest and vice versa. Sometimes people get caught up in the tiny details and they lose sight of the big picture and thus maybe another metaphor or ism would be sometimes you have to lose a couple of battles before you can win the war.

I think integrity is perhaps the most important. When people realize how much a real estate transaction happens without the client, without the client actually being in the room, and you think about all the conversations that happen with the other agent, with the attorney, with the inspector, starting the negotiation, your client has to know that when you are in the room, you are really advocating for their best interest and that takes a lot of trust.

Can you give a specific example of when these traits have played a role in your path towards success?

I can think of two or three that really stand out actually. One, it's a deal that it's some kind of odd to say, but I'm proud of not so much the outcome. I'm thrilled that the outcome went in our favor and my client is very happy or was very happy at the closing, but for me it was an incredible learning experience, and when you've been a real estate agent for 32 years, you would think, "Okay, well, what else could I possibly learn?"

But my client at the time is or was and is one of the top or is a top businessman in Chicago. He runs his firm. He's very tough to deal, but very fair, and is my buyer. The seller also a tough businessman and also a tough negotiator, and we started the negotiation process in October. We wrote an offer, submitted it, and we finished negotiating an agreement on terms in January and closed in February, and there were so many times during that deal where one side or the other was going to walk away. It looked like nothing was going to be able to or no one was going to be happy and the deal would fall apart, and then I would resurrect it, and to have both the buyer and sellers say to me that they were extremely impressed with my negotiating skills and credit me with keeping them both at the deal table to get to a closing, I felt really good about that.

What were some of the major adversities and trials that you had to overcome to achieve your goals?

I really can't, and I thought about this, and it's not that I have those stories of life, if any, I mean, I grew up with great brothers and parents and we certainly had a wonderful life, but we did not have a lot of money and we had a lot of struggles. My parents had a lot of struggles financially, but I just have a great memory of my childhood and I think that has stood me well because I can't say that I have any adversities that stood in my way or in my path to achieving goals or to being successful and I think actually some of the major adversities were just what I experienced as a child at what I saw my parents go through and it gave me in so many ways such an appreciation.

But also, when we work in an industry, at least in Chicago where we have a lot of expensive houses, people have gorgeous houses with beautiful finishes, and I remember my father once saying that what someone has on the outside, whether it's their house, their cars, their clothing, it doesn't define who they are. So, you try to find a way to be happy for people that have more than you and have empathy and compassion for someone who's struggling, but realize that those are all superficial, sort of outward appearances, and that doesn't define a person,

I think that sort of growing up with that and turning what could have been perceived as an adversity or a type of handy and being able to turn that around, I think that's a good quality. It certainly helps me in my business, and then I guess I'd have to speak to the downturn in the real estate market. A lot of agents that I think or that I felt were really good agents with the hope that they would be able to make it or stick the market out, but weren't able to, so I felt very fortunate that I was able to overcome some really bad years in the real estate world where we weren't making any money or a lot of us weren't making any money.

What kept you going despite these obstacles? Why didn't you give up?

If someone who is incredibly Type A and often described as rather a controlled freak, very controlling, I have a very Zen outlook on life, so I think that things are meant to be the way they're just meant to be, and everything comes at the right moment, be patient, so that's another. My daughter can tell you these isms are way too much, but there are some that I really lived by and one of them is that everything comes at the right moment, be patient, so I knew that this is something that had to happen and it was happening for a reason, and I just have to keep my head down and do my job and know that we were going to turn a corner at some point and not get bogged down on every deal, and when is the next deal going to come? It will come when it's supposed to and it worked.

Actually, when I think back in 2009, which, by all intents and purposes, would be considered a pretty dismal year, and I want to say that might have been the first or second-best year of my career.

What is your vision for your career for the next five years?

Every September I start planning for the following year, and I have a very specific way that I approach my business development and what goals I'm setting for the following year and I have a terrific, just an amazing managing broker here, and he spends a lot of time with me over those two months.

We just started that process and one of the things that I'm considering adding one of the business development ideas that we're talking about is as I call it dipping my talent to the team waters. I'm a single or solo agent, an individual agent, whatever that phrase would be, and I do have an executive assistant or admin assistant, I actually have two, and they're fantastic.

But I have a couple of agents that have from time to time helps me or I spend send some business their way and there's a synergy. We discovered this synergy between the five of us that is really special, and we find that we all fit together in the office, even though three of those people don't have designated areas, and I've sat down with each of those, each of the four people and my managing broker, and I'm just exploring and maybe we become a team and I can see how from a business development perspective, certainly I could do substantially more volume and more transactions if I have more help.

But I also see a number of teams that are really structured to do more business not necessarily working as a finely tuned team or machine, but it's all about developing volume that it all goes under one individual agent's name, and that's not the kind of team I've ever looked at wanting to be. It's not bad. There's no bad or good, it's just I think you have to set your business plan up to work for you and to be authentic for you as an agent.

But I'm very intrigued and it seems to me that there could be a lot of benefits to my clients, and that would be the first and foremost reason I would implement a business development initiative, but that's something that's at the forefront. So maybe by 2017, we'll be – I don't know what we'll call ourselves, but maybe the Dobbs Team.

What do you feel is the best way you market yourself as a real estate professional for continual growth?

I think it's all about personal communication and picking up the phone and written notes, networking with my professional peers and my professional associates. There's a lot of social media and search engine optimization. I have someone on my team or one of my staff that does marketing and specifically search engine optimization and social media, and that is a way of growing one's business and certainly, it brings in leads, but I think to differentiate myself as a real estate agent and really market me as opposed to developing business, I think that that takes personal, it's the one on one.

What's the biggest misconception/myth people have about working with a real estate agent?

There's the impression that agents are all about their commission first, and when I think people think that we're overpaid. I don't think that either of those is true. At least they're not true in my case, and again, I work with some really, really amazing smart people that are tops in their profession and they've said anything but that. I mean, a good agent knows that you're in this for the long haul and if you approach your business based on the individual deal, you'll never make it.

If you were to get a call from a family member in another state, wanting to sell their home, what advice would you give them about selecting an agent that can best serve their needs?

Well, I didn't tell you what I do, I pretend when I travel sometimes if it's a market that I'm interested in, because every time I'm on vacation, no matter where I'm always interested in the real estate market. I sort of go with this approach that, "Well, if I were going to buy or sell a house here, what would I do?"

And this is the advice that I would give upfront to a family member. I would visit open houses and let's say I'm in a community and I have a house in where there are signs out on the street of a single family home. You go visit open houses and get to meet some agents. I mean, one way to find an agent is to meet someone in an open house, and if they're doing a really good job and they are acting in a way that if you have an agent sitting at your house for an open house, that's how you would want your agent to present themselves on your property. I think that's a good indicator to at least getting the name of someone that you might interview or further explore.

Also, you can ask friends. If any of your friends have recently bought or sold, do they have a good experience with their agents? But I would take it one step beyond that if you ask someone and the answer is yes, and then why. Because sometimes, and this is why there's a different fit between, you know. There can be an agent that works well with one particular client and maybe not so well with another or vice versa, and that is everyone has a different set of expectations and a way that they work and communicate, so it's important that that fit, and that to me, the fit between the agent and the client is as important as the professional credentials of the real estate agent. So, asking someone, if they had a good experience and then why will help you know if the why matches what would be important to you in picking your agent.

How can someone that needs a real estate agent find out more about you and how you can help?

I would love for them to call me and they can have my phone number or visit my website. If someone were to go on my website, debradobbs.com, they would find everything. I mean, I have a blog with blog posts. I'm very into the 77 neighborhoods of Chicago, and I have a whole section of just about Chicago's neighborhoods and what I love about them and then some data points and lots of client testimonials. But if someone wants to get to know me, just pick up the phone and call.

Top Agent Maria Cedano

Maria Cedano, of RE/MAX Ultimate Professionals, is based out of Shorewood, Illinois. Maria is fluent in English and Spanish with 19 years of real estate experience. She has been named by REAL Trends as one of America's Best Real Estate Agents for 2016. She has also been recognized by the National Association of Hispanic Real Estate Professionals (NAHREP) as one of the Top 250 Latino Agents in the country for 2016. She is also a Realtor liaison for the national builder, CalAtlantic, for the communities of Hunters Ridge and Greywall Club in Joliet.

What led you to real estate? Was it something that you always knew that you wanted to do?

I always was interested in real estate, but I actually began in my career because of the schedule it allows for me and my family. We lived on a property and I needed a flexible schedule with small children at home and this was something that was ideal for me at that time. Daytime appointments when I wasn't available were referred out to someone full time and I started on a part-time basis and now has been doing it for 23 years.

What personal attributes, traits or qualities have most contributed to your success and how did you develop these?

I've always been a person that is early to bed and early to rise, and I still remember the old saying, "The early bird catches the worm," and being present is the most important thing. I think I like getting up early and going to work and feeling that sense of accomplishment early on in the day to fill the rest of the day, and it has helped me out quite a bit.

Can you give a specific example of when these traits have played a role in your path towards success?

Many times, people work 9 to 5 and they'll dial the phone or send an email assuming they'll get voicemail or that their answers would be responded to at some point during the day, and I'm able to respond quickly, so in that response has helped me out a lot. I catch it before it rang out and I'm able to respond and if I don't know the answers, I have time during the morning to get those questions answered or the information that's needed and then get back to them in a very timely manner, and so that has helped me out quite a bit.

What were some of the major adversities and trials that you had to overcome to achieve your goals?

Basically, the hardest part was learning to balance family with career, especially starting off when I had small children at home, which are now grown and out, but scheduling appointments and trying to meet my appointments in a timely manner required a lot of discipline, and with that said, that was fairly the hardest part in the beginning.

But there's a man I've been fortunate enough to have that helped and a strong will to succeed, and being a workaholic has also helped me quite a bit. I've put in long hours and it works, it helps. People know that they can reach me, that they can find me that I will find out whatever they need to know and get back to them quickly.

What kept you going despite these obstacles? Why didn't you give up?

I was fortunate enough to have a great core team around me. My brokers have been available for any questions, and of course, at home, my husband and my family have been wonderful. They make sure that things get done when I'm not there and I know I had that piece of mind and I was able to give a 100% with whatever I was doing. So, I would have to say my support system.

What is your vision for your career for the next five years?

My vision is to create a better team. Of course, technology these days is the best way to go, so we're constantly working and bringing in new technology, new avenues, ease of use for the consumers so that we can get back to them in the way that we traditionally have done by phone or by email also through apps and different applications that are out there and implementing those into our systems. With a great support system, around me and a great office team, we are getting there and we constantly grow.

What do you feel is the best way you market yourself as a real estate professional for continual growth?

I'm combining modern technology with old-fashioned footwork. I still do the flyers. I still meet people at off hours. I do go to my local businesses and meet the proprietors. I still go to the local banks and introduce myself to new clients. I try to join memberships. We do a lot of fundraising. I do donations through every transaction to different locations so that they know we're here, we're making money and we'll sort of contributing back to the community. I think we're merging technology and old-fashioned footwork very well and I hope to keep being able to do that in the future.

What's the biggest misconception/myth people have about working with a real estate agent?

I think the biggest misconception is that they can do it themselves. In terms of working with an agent, I think that sometimes the public thinks that we just open the door whenever, but there are a lot of legal regulations, disclosures, a lot of liabilities that go in with our processing and I think that people would be surprised, if they haven't used an agent in the past, how much work goes into it and hopefully they're happy with it.

A misconception that we don't work weekends and that we're hard to get a hold of is really not the case in most of our area. We work 10- to 12-hour days and we're happy to do so. We're available, we're locals and we do enough business to keep ourselves surrounded with good help and good assistants. Our offices are actually growing so that tells me that we're doing something good and the idea of doing an honest job and the money will follow, and that has proven itself time and time again. Sometimes we don't get paid and that's okay too. I mean, you just basically put in an honest day's work and everything works out fine after that.

If you were to get a call from a family member in another state, wanting to sell their home, what advice would you give them about selecting an agent that can best serve their needs?

They need to have an advocate. I work dual agents in Indiana and Illinois for quite a while and I did get a call from a family member this morning and basically what I told him was find a local agent, a real estate is local, and even though there is accessibility on the web and everything in technology allows you to work from a distance, I would still work with someone local because you do need that combination. You need someone who works full time, someone who's going to be there for you, someone who can actually make it in a timely fashion and someone you can rely on.

I would say check their references. With technology, it's really easy to reach out to their past clients and find out, "Were you happy? What is it they do? What did they not do best?" Even though no one is perfect, it will give you an idea of what you're stepping into from the consumer's point of view.

How can someone that needs a real estate agent find out more about you and how you can help?

They can log onto my website, which is mcedano.illinoisproperty.com. They can also find me on the National Hispanics Registry. I am bilingual. Realtor.com, Zillow, and all the public sites also have links to my website so they could also call my cell phone, 815-560-1585.

Top Agent Alan Wang

Alan Wang of Alan Wang Realty Group at Keller Williams Realty based out of Campbell, California has been a realtor in the San Francisco Bay Area since 2003 and is currently with Keller Williams Realty. He ranks in the top 1% of all Keller Williams' agents in Northern California and Hawaii and is a member of the Agent Leadership Council and a trainer and mentor. He has been in the technology industry for over 14 years with roles in engineering, project program, product management and business development.

What led you to real estate? Was it something that you always knew that you wanted to do?

I stumbled into it. I was actually in the technology industry and had a good career going there. I did notice some layoffs coming around the 2000 timeframe so I decided to have a parallel track and a backup plan. Never in my imagination have I thought that it would blossom into a thriving business, and so I decided to quit my job in tech and shift it over.

What personal attributes, traits or qualities have most contributed to your success and how did you develop these?

It's one of these industries where is different in corporate America. Corporate America is often who you know, not what you know. In real estate, it's the opposite. It's really about what you know. I mean, definitely, there's an aspect of relationships, but really one thing would be hard work. In hard work, some folks use the word "hustle," just getting things done and just working harder than the agent next to you.

I get up at 6:30 a.m. and I sleep at 1 a.m., and I'm just catching up with clients and meeting with clients or trying to manage things, and for every ounce of hard work I've put in, the results show, and that's what I love about this business. If it is one thing, I would say hard work.

Can you give a specific example of when these traits have played a role in your path towards success?

Day in day out, I mean, people would look at our team and they'd go, "Wow! They're doing so well." I mean, they don't really realize today I was at a sign off right before this meeting and the title agent told me, "I really appreciate you being here. Most agents don't bother showing up." And that's one of those things that I really tie myself on.

It's not just hard work, but it's just doing the right thing, giving the person a great experience, being there for them when they expect you to be there. At sign off, yes, it's correct, the agents are not required to be there, for example, but imagine if you were a buyer or seller sitting there staring at a stranger across from you not knowing what you're signing, you're signing your life away, whether you're buying or selling, and that's an example of where I think just, you know. The hard work is still in there and just doing the right thing is really what I pride myself on.

What were some of the major adversities and trials that you had to overcome to achieve your goals?

I'd break it down in two ways. One thing I've had to deal with is tough markets and the second is tough clients. We'll start with tough markets. In the 30 years, I've been doing this, there have been a couple of times when the market sort of took a nosedive. The first time would be after the year 2000 when the dot-com bust happened and the second time will be around the 2005 thing with the subprime meltdown happened, and those are really tough times.

I mean, talking about tough markets, we had coworkers will work in the mall trying to make ends meet. I mean, the rest of the years have been good, but there are a couple of bad ones, and I think in those tough markets, we have a phrase, "You work the market that you're in."

I heard a lot of people complain about "the market is terrible, there's nothing to sell." I mean, if you're in a bad market, then you'd just kind of get into stressed fields, for example. You're just going to have to go and find out and figure out how to work those. They're not easy, but you're just going to have to learn, and so I think really learning to adapt to tough market, and I think the agents that survived are the ones that are just going to work with what's in front of them, so that's the first one, it's the tough market.

The second one I would say is tough clients, and if that's a really tough clients at times to manage, and it's one of these things where I would say, as early in your career, you don't always have a choice of who you can work with and so that you work with everybody. I'd rather say as the business starts thriving, I mean, you can actually have a choice, and some clients, I mean, those that don't value you as an agent, they don't value what you bring to the table, they're continually negotiating and giving you a hard time, and those clients, for me, I mean, if I do have to work with them, I just have to just put in my mind that I have to deal what's best for them. But if I don't have to work with them, I'll often choose not to because it's just not a cultural fit, and so those are the ways that I've dealt with and overcome these obstacles.

What kept you going despite these obstacles? Why didn't you give up?

The primary one, survival would be a good one. You've got to work to survive, and that's definitely a very strong motivator. But at the same time, I mean, just being able to adapt. Currently, the market is great. Everything is just looking upwards, but I'm already gearing up for the next shift in the marketplace. It's probably two to three years away, but I'm preparing myself for it, and the reason I do that is because when things get tough, you could just quit or you could just figure it out and challenge yourself on how you weather the storm, and I like the challenge. Obviously, survival is one thing. You've got to feed your family, but beyond that, I mean, I just don't want to quit. I never want to quit. It's just always I have to figure out a way, and therein lies the challenge, and challenge really makes like more interesting rather than just throwing in the towel and giving up.

What is your vision for your career for the next five years?

It's interesting when I started this business, it's a very long time, over a decade, I was doing it by myself. I live and did everything by myself. These last couple of years, I've been really just putting the business mindset on and putting that business head on and saying, "All right, this is not scalable. I'm not going to be able to do everything forever."

I just see myself as really, I am truly kind of a CEO of my company. I'm the person at the top and yes, I may work with certain clients, et cetera, but really I want to have a team, a strong team, where the buyers are assigned, if they're looking, they're assigned, an operational team supporting them, and for me, I want to focus on the strategy of the company, the direction that we're going and be a thought leader in the industry and really pushing onto that way and just really manage the team and lead team, inspire the team, motivate the team, but not necessarily be in the day today, because one of the things I've seen with agents that have been doing real estate too long is that it's a grueling business and I see customer service go down, the agents don't want to answer the phone anymore. They don't want to talk anymore with agents. They don't want to do any more of that anymore, and it's understandable, because you're burned out, and I don't even want to be anywhere close to that. I definitely want to have a team, a strong team in place so that we continue to have great experiences for our customers.

What do you feel is the best way you market yourself as a real estate professional for continual growth?

I don't think I believe on this next wave. I think in the past, realtors have done a lot of different lead generation methodologies. I mean, you could do call calling, do the door knocking. Of course, there's always the relationship and referral business, lots of perspective. I think this new generation, Millennials, are looking for something else. They don't answer their phones so you can't cold call them. You can try to text them, but there is so much noise that you have to bring something of value before they're looking to you.

Basically, the question is, why should anybody be looking to you as an agent, and basically, what I'm calling it is every agent should be a subject matter expert, but what I mean is that people identify you as somebody who is an expert in real estate and they want to read your material, they want to call you, they want to watch your videos and hear your message and your opinion on the subject, and I think that's really the future. That's the way I go about it.

I do heavy blogging on LinkedIn, which is a professional network than Facebook, but professional, and that's where everyone's professional connections are, and so I do try to really put out good, solid real estate content that people will be able to consume that, and it's not really about marketing, but it's about how can I give you something of value, and sooner, of course, you're going to visualize and see me as an expert. That's a byproduct of it.

But really, I'm just going to be a giving person that's giving as much as I know and spread the knowledge out and also, again, as a side effect, yes, it is marketing, but I really want it to be less about marketing, but I'm just a giving person and providing an expert opinion on something and just people will actually go, "Hey, if I'll need anything, I'm going to call Alan with this thing," and that's really kind of the next wave I'm trying to push with this content marketing as being a subject matter expert in this space.

What's the biggest misconception/myth people have about working with a real estate agent?

I think a lot of folks sort of view real estate agents as folks who are just kind of that cliché of the sleazy car salesman, the used car salesmen, right? Again, no offense to anyone who's a car salesman, but there's always that image when you go into a dealership that, "Oh, I don't want to talk to that person. Oh gosh, I don't think that they're giving it away. It's confrontation. They're not looking for us." And I think a lot of people, you can see that same attitude when they walk into open houses and they don't really want to talk to you. They don't want to give you any information. It's because of that perception that we're this big salesperson, and it doesn't help that our license says real estate salesperson either.

However, I really think that's a myth. I think if you look at the core of the business, it's usually relationship driven. What I mean by that is your realtor would most likely be somebody that you know and you trust, and so that trust is key. Without that, then everything is a great step, and so once that trust is set, the agent, they're not to sell you something. I mean, a house is going to vary. The average price of the house is a million dollars. So, no matter how good a salesperson I am, I'm not going to be able to sell you a house that you don't like, that you're not going to love, you and your wife or you or your spouse or your family or other.

No matter how good a salesman I am, I may be able to pressure you into it at the moment, but you're going home, "Oh, you know, this house is not for me,' and you're going to say no, and so really, I think what buyers and sellers and brokers understand is that we're partners in this business. We're not going to sell you anything. That's not our job. We have a fiduciary duty to do what's best for you, act in your best interest as a buyer or seller, and based on that we need to operate in that fashion and we're not going to sell you anything that you're not going to buy.

I know a lot of agents come to a listing appointment and they're ready to make somebody sign on the dotted line. Well, that's fine as an approach, but if I force and pester you to sign, the moment you change your mind later, really, we want people to work with us for the long term.

It has to be a mutual decision between the both of us, so high-pressure tactics and all, I'm not a fan of them. I think you're really going to work with my team or not and it's all about the relationship, and I think, for me, that's why I never envision myself as a salesperson.

Sure, I have a component of sales. I have to do marketing on your home for you and set up great brochures and websites and doing tours and all that good stuff, but that's not necessarily mean I need to be high pressure, sleazy salesperson. I don't think that's a myth that you should go with.

If you were to get a call from a family member in another state, wanting to sell their home, what advice would you give them about selecting an agent that can best serve their needs?

What I do is that each real estate agents are their own startup company really in our own little businesses, and every time I found a member, I'd ask him, "How would you differentiate yourself from other agents?" That's one question I would have to ask and I'd sit back and wait and listen. I mean, really, what I was trying to hear is what is this agent's elevator pitch? In two or three sentences, what makes them different, and every agent should have one of these because every day when you walk and running, you're going to meet somebody who's going to ask you, "What do you do for a living, and then they're going to ask you, "Oh, well, a realtor, okay, well, what makes you different?" And I think that's probably a really good screening question, just sit back and listen. If they don't have an answer, what makes them different, then you just try to move on, and I think it's easy to get a license, but if their interest is extremely low and if the first thing out of their mouth is, "Well, we do, you know, or something," then they have really devalued themselves. They have nothing else to say but give you a discount right away, as an example.

Some good answers from agents would be, I guess you could tell your steps. I mean, that's one way. The second one would be if you're selling a home, "These are the ten things I do to market your house that most agents don't bother with." Do you do Facebook ads? Do you do drone videos? Do you do e-tours? Do you have high-quality top people for your flyers? What makes you different? Everyone else's can put a house in MLS. That's not a differentiating. Everyone else says, "Yeah, everything is online." Well, that's not difficult anymore. I'm there for my clients. I'm a person of high integrity. Everybody is like that. So, I think really figure out what differentiate this agent.

Now, of course, they have to mesh with you as the buyer or seller. It has to be a cultural fit. Now, you may not value certain things in the certain agent, so you have to pick one that's a cultural fit for you.

How can someone that needs a real estate agent find out more about you and how you can help?

Our website would be the best, www.alanwangrealty.com, and of course, you can reach me directly if you like, 408-313-4352, but yes, our website is the best place for much information about our listings, our blogs, our videos, and everything, a lot of resources to help you there.

Top Agent Melanie Giglio-Vakos

Melanie Giglio-Vakos of Jameson Sotheby's International Realty is based out of Chicago, Illinois. Melanie has been in the real estate industry for over fifteen years and she is not afraid to say that she is constantly learning and growing in an industry she loves. She is proud to say that she has been consistently in the top 1% of Realtors for the past seven years and just recently, she and her team (MVP Team) became the top performers for all of Sotheby's International in Chicago. A celebrated media moment for Melanie was the Crain's coverage of the most expensive resale transaction in Trump Tower last year where she represented the buyer, a long-time client.

What led you to real estate? Was it something that you always knew that you wanted to do?

Throughout my life, I've always been in the sales and the service industry in one way or another, and I was just very fortunate that at a very young age, I was able to purchase my first home and it was not a very pretty experience. I was just going through this really bad experience during what I thought was supposed to be a very exciting time and it was kind of that defining moment when I knew that a career in real estate was probably the path that I was meant to pursue.

I just wanted to make sure that doing it that I was doing everything in my power as a real estate professional that I could ensure that my client experience was very positive from the very beginning to the very end, unlike the experience that I had. So being involved in the transaction of people's homes often, it's just the largest and the most important asset, I want to guide them through the entire process in the system and making all the best choices of all the things that I knew that I would be good at.

I knew that it was having a great understanding of people and really listening to their wants and needs and desires from which all are very necessary for a successful transaction, and therefore, a very successful real estate professional, and I knew at that time I was a perfect fit for the industry.

What personal attributes, traits or qualities have most contributed to your success and how did you develop these?

Sales, it's always been a part of my life. From the lemonade stand that I made at eight years old, which I must say the most profitable in the neighborhood, to selling random items throughout my school and college years. Gosh, there's a huge list of things that I've sold, but it's been in my blood and I just believe being a good salesperson is more of an innate skill and you could certainly learn some sales techniques, but the art of selling is something that I believe that you're either born with or not. I feel like selling is an art, and it's an art of building long-term relationships, building trust and ultimately having a keen understanding of just human behavior.

I'm a believer, and I'm constantly learning from the best in the industry, and with that, I'm constantly attending seminars, conferences, and I do have some very few important mentors in my life.

Can you give a specific example of when these traits have played a role in your path towards success?

Well, like I said, from a very early time in my life, I felt like I was always selling and one way or another. I mean, I sold Mary Kay. I even remember selling lollipops when I was in 7th grade. It's just like I've always been in sales. When I got a little bit older, I worked at the mall in all the store selling clothes. Every job that I've ever had in my life from, I would say, eight years old, I've always done some form of selling, and so that was just something that I knew that I needed to do. I just figured at some point in my life that I was going to sell the most important thing in people's lives, their most important asset. So that's how I got into it.

What were some of the major adversities and trials that you had to overcome to achieve your goals?

Two definitely come to mind. I'd say that my major adversities that were, unfortunately, and fortunately, surviving the financial crisis of 2008 and I had breast cancer in 2012. So, when the financial markets crashed, I knew that I basically had no choice, but to do what I had to do to survive in real estate. So, I was fortunate enough to have the opportunity to join an REO seminar, a foreclosure seminar, and become one of Chicago banks' like go-to realtors for dealing with their foreclosure transactions, so this is really how I was able to survive in real estate.

Then also while I was going through my treatments for breast cancer, the few precious hours that I actually had, when I was feeling well enough to work and focus on it, I just made sure that I use them wisely. Even if there's only an hour to a day, I made sure that I really narrow down exactly what I needed to focus on in order to have a successful work day, and by this point, I've been in real estate for over ten-plus years and I created a database that I was really proud of. So, I worked my database and my network from my bed and I did all that I could to prepare so that when I was ready, I had the business lined up, and with that, 2012 ended up being my best year at that point.

What kept you going despite these obstacles? Why didn't you give up?

Giving up was never an option for me. It just wasn't in my DNA. In 2011, right before I got diagnosed with breast cancer, I had my beautiful daughter, Aria, and I fought for her during my ordeal with cancer.

What is your vision for your career for the next five years?

I see myself continuing to work. I feel like I'm always going to work, but at a level that I will only be nurturing my relationships that I fostered over the past twenty years and that I've empowered my team to handle the day-to-day operations of the business. We're called the MVP Team, and I just want the MVP Team to be number one in the country, and I have no doubt that we'll achieve that goal.

What do you feel is the best way you market yourself as a real estate professional for continual growth?

Well, honestly, the way that I feel like I am constantly marketing myself is not necessarily much more than just constantly calling my database of past clients and sphere of influence and reminding them that I'm out there selling real estate, and that is truly what I feel has been my huge success. I'll reach the pinnacle of success when my database has become my number one vehicle for business. I have an incredible database, and I'm constantly getting fed referrals from it.

What's the biggest misconception/myth people have about working with a real estate agent?

I would probably say that this is what I hear that we just provide no value, and they could simply just use the internet or for sale by owners' situation, they think it's that easy, and I think it's completely false. Anyone that has that mentality, I am very happy and willing to meet at my beautiful Gold Coast office and give a formal presentation.

If you were to get a call from a family member in another state, wanting to sell their home, what advice would you give them about selecting an agent that can best serve their needs?

You know what, I get this all the time actually. I just had one recently where I had my past client sold their place and they're moving to Denver. So basically, the first thing that I do, I called the Sotheby's International Realty office in New York City and I would ask for the best agent that's suited for that particular transaction and I'm really fortunate that Sotheby's has an incredible national and international referral program so that I know that when I refer someone to a counterpart in another city, that they'll be handled with the same level of care and professionalism that I handle with all my clients.

How can someone that needs a real estate agent find out more about you and how you can help?

They are welcome to reach out to me anytime. My email address, my direct email address is Melanie@melaniegiglio.com, and/or they can just call me. Call me on my cellphone, 312-953-4998. My team and I, pretty much, we work 24/7 so we're always going to help.

Top Agent Sue Hall

Sue Hall, of Century 21 Elm Realtors is based out of Park Ridge, Illinois. Sue has been in real estate for the past 32 years, and 30 of those have been with Century 21 Elm in Park Ridge. She has been a consistent top producer, and in 2015, she finished # 1 in the State of Illinois for Century 21. She has also been awarded the Chicago Magazine-sponsored 5-Star Agent Award since its inception in 2011. As a former teacher, she still finds real estate, after 32 years, to be an exciting profession.

What led you to real estate? Was it something that you always knew that you wanted to do?

It's probably more of a stumble. I used to be a teacher and I taught for about seven years, and there were just a lot of changes when I first started teaching at that time and job shortages.

So, a good friend of mine had been in real estate and he said, "You know, you might want to try it." I said, "Oh." I remember when I was a kid traveling with my grandfather to open houses on Sunday as an activity, and I used to hate it, and I thought, "Oh, no, I don't think so." And he said, "Well, why don't you just give it a try one summer before you go back to school in September."

And that's what I did. I walked into a real estate company in Park Ridge. At the time I was living in Chicago, Park Ridge is a suburb that backs up to Chicago. So I walked in there and it looked like a lot of successful people sitting at nice desk and I just walked in and said I wanted to be in real estate, and they all said, "Come on in," and trained me and I took the real estate class in probably about a month and I was able to make a couple of sales right away prior to going back to school in September, and that probably equaled what I was making at the time, so at that moment I gave up teaching and went into real estate.

What personal attributes, traits or qualities have most contributed to your success and how did you develop these?

I think teaching helps a lot, and I know a lot of former teachers in the real estate business. The ability to multitask, that's a part and parcel of a teacher's job. You might have a lesson plan in front of you, but suddenly somebody in the back of the room faints or somebody else is hitting somebody with a ruler or something happens and you're constantly distracted and kind of taken off the track.

I kind of sometimes equate that with real estate. I might start my day out thinking I have a couple of appointments early nothing light, and by the end of the day, I have things that are filled in and are going all day. So, I think you really have to be very, very flexible and be able to multitask to do it properly.

What were some of the major adversities and trials that you had to overcome to achieve your goals?

I think that I started out in a town that I didn't live in. I have lived in a city and I somehow was shopping in Park Ridge and just kind of fell into looking at a real estate office there, it was just dumb luck. I didn't realize that I didn't know the streets, I didn't know the schools. I didn't know anything about the town, and when I started there, there were a lot of us to go, so I had to learn a whole new community, and probably in hindsight, that wasn't the smartest thing at the time to do, but I was young and this is my 32nd year, so I was young enough to be able to kind of just roll with it and I didn't have children at the time. I didn't have anything holding me back from working a lot of hours at the beginning in order to kind of achieve those goals and try to learn as much as I could about the community.

But I made myself available to everyone. After I got my license, I went into some of the top agents in the office and I said, "Whenever you go out on a presentation, can I come with you. Whenever you are presenting an offer," and in those days, we used to present offers face to face, "I'd like to just come with and observe."

So probably the very first year I did lots of observation and kind of found my own style. There were some people that maybe were more direct, some were more laid back and I sort of was able to develop my own style in presenting and working. I also had, although it wasn't an obstacle because I didn't know anything, I was also much younger than anyone else in the business at that time.

The town, probably the median age in those days, the real estate agent was probably like 55 in this community, so I was in my late 20s, so I was kind of stood out in that respect, and that was good for me because I had the energy to do a lot of running around, but it was bad because I had to win over a lot of people that had been in the business for a long time and weren't used to that kind of change.

What kept you going despite these obstacles? Why didn't you give up?

Number one, I enjoyed the business. I liked working with people. The whole idea of doing the best job that I could do for someone in finding a house which is one of the biggest things most people do in their lives, I really, really enjoyed the dealing with people one on one.

Secondly, I liked the flexibility of the job. I liked to be able to, although I work probably more weekends than everybody, I'd like just being able to plan my day sometimes differently than when I had a regular 9 to 5 job, and of course, the compensation, the monetary compensation was there. I started making probably more money than I could ever make teaching in those years, and it was appealing to me, and I also liked starting a project and finishing it, and not having seemed kind of left out there. I kind of like working through something through the whole process and having a completely finished and starting something new.

So, it just was a good fit for me all the way around for my personality and just for the career move and the drive that I had at the time, it was just a perfect fit for me in real estate.

What is your vision for your career for the next five years?

My business has been growing rapidly, especially over the past three or four years. I think since the recession and we've kind of made a little bit of a comeback, at least our market is getting stronger, I feel that there are less real estate agents in the business and the ones that are standing after going through the recession period are the ones that are doing the majority of the business now, and I think because of my longevity in the town, again, my 32nd year, I feel that people recognize me and more and more people are contacting me.

So, I feel that in the next three to five years with some new technologies, with television, with the videos that I'm doing, some of the websites that I'm involved in, I just feel like my business can just grow by leaps and bounds, but I think the thing is, we have to change. We have to go with the technology. I mean, when I started in the business, the country used carbon paper underneath, but now we're emails, texts, Twitter, blogs. We have to move with the changing market, and because of that and some assistant hope that I have that's very, very good, I just feel that the next three to five years, my business could possibly double.

What do you feel is the best way you market yourself as a real estate professional for continual growth?

Probably the ability to buy into a lot of websites that are very popular, and Zillow, Realtor.com, Homes.com, Trulia, I've kind of entrenched myself buying out the zip codes, things like that, so I'm the agent that comes up when most people are doing their searches, and I've gone to some video work where I can have my listings videoed and put on the computer. We're on Comcast in the real estate section of Park Ridge, and on demand on television, I can showcase some of my listings there and open myself up to a whole new set of buyers, and it's been very successful. Plus, I've done regular marketing tasks in the town I'm in via Shopping Cart, ads in the paper, just putting myself out there and making myself as visible as possible.

What's the biggest misconception/myth people have about working with a real estate agent?

I think they think it's just easy to sell a house, and in some cases, it is easy. You could put a sign-out and the house can sell right away, but that's only half of what goes on. There are so many other parts to a puzzle with attorneys, inspections, documenting things, following up any kind of problems on disclosures. Right now, we face problems with flooding, radon, asbestos, molds. These are things that happen almost daily in my business. I have to find out and I have to know who to call for a remediation. I have to know what to do on certain inspection issues, and a lot of times, it's just keeping all the people involved in the transaction, kind of calm in talking, and that's where people's tempers are rising.

I do a lot of psychological work all day just talking to people trying to keep everybody's tempers under control and just trying to make sure that everybody realizes that we're all working towards a common goal and that's to get the house closed. A lot of times buyers and sellers don't always get along and you have to kind of play interference there so that you can keep the deal moving smoothly and we don't get egos involved and suddenly it blows up over nothing. Selling the house is one thing, but keeping it together and taking it all the way to the closing is quite another thing.

If you were to get a call from a family member in another state, wanting to sell their home, what advice would you give them about selecting an agent that can best serve their needs?

I definitely think it has to be somebody local. I think with the inception of the internet in real estate, people now list properties all over, 50 miles, 100 miles from where they're at. I don't think that that's the best use of the real estate agent. I think to find somebody local, someone, in your direct area that does a lot of business, and again, listing, working with buyers, but it has to be somebody local who understands the community, the schools, any other problems, and just things like where's the library, what kind of theaters do you have, what kind of health clubs are available, what are the concerts in the park, what is that about.

There are so many parts of the community, so getting somebody that's local and understands the community and the area and the values for that matter. In the northwest suburb of Chicago, but if somebody came from 100 miles away, they may not understand the value of this community because they have a different pricing structure in their community for the same kind of house. Getting a local professional is probably my best advice to those people.

How can someone that needs a real estate agent find out more about you and how you can help?

They can contact me. I'm at Century 21 Elm Realtors in Park Ridge. The number is 847-692-5522 and my direct line is 847-917-3188, and they can also look up my bio on Google, of course.

Top Agent Megan Aitken

Megan Aitken, of Megan Aitken Group at Keller Williams Realty is based out of Middletown, Delaware. In 2003, Megan got her start in new home sales with a Fortune 500 homebuilder selling new construction in the Baltimore market. After achieving Rookie of the Year and setting regional sales records, Megan was quickly offered a transfer opportunity in Middletown, Delaware to sell in a growing market. When Megan determined she would be happier representing the client rather than the builder, she obtained her real estate license and went out on her own.

Since 2012 she has been awarded by Five Star Professional three years in a row as a 5-star real estate agent for client satisfaction, and she's been featured in Delaware Today Magazine as a "Top Agent" in Delaware. From closing one home in 2012, this year Megan has closed 68 homes totaling 17 million in sales, 90% of which were within the Middletown area.

What led you to real estate? Was it something that you always knew that you wanted to do?

Actually, I did kind of stumble into it. Pretty young I got out of college looking for a job in sales and I happen to go to a job fair where there was full of national homebuilders that were seeking college grads to sell some new construction homes, and I interviewed for two and I ended up given a position with a Fortune 500 homebuilder and the love was instant with them and the connection I had with my clients just made me fall in love with the general in general, and that's where I got my start in selling new homes.

What personal attributes, traits or qualities have most contributed to your success and how did you develop these?

My parents will tell you I was born with a bit of a headstrong personality and I've been determined throughout most of my life to basically motivate myself to get things accomplished, and that has driven me in all of my aspects of my life to get things accomplished, whether it was in school or in my career or in my job, and I definitely feel that it has been a huge aspect of my contributions towards my success.

Can you give a specific example of when these traits have played a role in your path towards success?

A great example would be after about six years in the new construction business and after I was pregnant with our twins, I took a quick time out to stay home and raise the twins, and I decided to go back into real estate with my real estate license and get out of new construction and start my business out in the field on my own, and I really had to start my business from zero switching from new construction over to being out in the field as a real estate agent and that, in fact, required me to completely self-motivate myself to build my brand, build my business, use some of that headstrong capabilities that I had from growing up and really motivate myself to get up, get out there and just build relationships with people and get the word out there that I was on my own and that I just really wanted to have this business on my own and that was what propelled me into being able to retain clients and get referrals and get the word of that out there.

What were some of the major adversities and trials that you had to overcome to achieve your goals?

One of the biggest trials I would say was trying to be a mom, and a working mom at that, with having three young kids and trying to get back out in the business. My husband works at that time and I was super determined to have my business up and running. I would say time management was probably one of my biggest hardships at the time, I think, with just trying to juggle everything.

My son, one of the twins, was diagnosed with autism at the young age of two, so I was actually trying to get him up to his therapies while also trying to manage my schedule. While I'm showing homes, I would take my kids with me on my showing, actually taking them into the properties or wherever I needed to be, I would have them with me just to accomplish what I needed to accomplish that.

Time management sure was the biggest challenge at the time, but I did what I needed to do. I had the support that I needed from my family to get it done, but it's just that that's the self-determination in trying to accomplish that goal, the end goal, in sight that drives you to get through it.

Sometimes I look back, I don't know how I did that, but you kind of do what needs to be done to survive at the time, and it was certainly quite a time for me, but it was an enjoyable time at that as well.

What kept you going despite these obstacles? Why didn't you give up?

A lot of the times people would tell me like, "Are you crazy? What are doing, you're so busy and you have so much going on?"

But the truth is I was so honored and motivated by the clients and their responses to me and their thankfulness and just the compliments they would give me and the things they would say to enrich my life in return was rewarding, and they motivated me to be a better realtor and to become better at what I did.

They sent me their families, they sent me their friends, they sent me their cousins, uncles, neighbors and they kept me so busy and their experiences were so good with me that it was almost as if they just weren't getting that kind of experience from anyone else and it just blew my mind that there just wasn't another agent that was able to offer them that experience, and that just made me want to give more people that kind of client experience with the knowledge and client care that I was able to give.

So I was very motivated by their responses, but I also can't get off of that question without giving the credit also to the support and encouragement I got from my husband who if he hadn't been so good and obviously just encouraged me to get up when I was down or told me to get out of the door on a weekend, he would take care of the kids and I could go out and show houses all weekend when obviously, he's juggling his work as well and he was very encouraging and very supportive when we were very busy.

I think at the same time, it takes a whole team to be able to support a lifestyle like this when you have a very chaotic schedule, but I think what encouraged me not to give up was just seeing the smiling faces of the clients at the end of the closings and the fact that they would send me and trust me with their families and friends, there was no way or there wasn't even an option to give up, but giving up was never an option for me.

What is your vision for your career for the next five years?

I've been very fortunate to have had the opportunity to bring on a full-time licensed assistant the past year, which has allowed me to grow in my business the past year. We have more than doubled our clientele in just twelve months and we're looking to continue this growth within the area. The area in our town is growing. We have one of the fastest-growing areas in the county and a lot is happening around here. We're trying to continue to grow and invest in the community and have a business because I want to better serve them.

I want to continue to see my team give back to the community and potentially then see if I can even expand with some more agents. Well, I get very particular obviously like with very good client care, but my clients know that I am like that, so, therefore, I would make sure I have agents that can give that client care, but to grow my team and make sure that I can give enough of me back out to the clients that are looking for service and help within the community. The community is looking to expand within a school district system so I'm looking to try to help within that expansion and try to push the referendum that is just going out there, help within the local fundraisers that go out, and I'm just excited for what's happening here in this town in the next five years.

What do you feel is the best way you market yourself as a real estate professional for continual growth?

I have really saturated myself in this town as I've moved here eleven years ago. Now, I've lived here and my family has been raised here and I have really saturated myself in the town knowledge and the schools and the area and just in general, I want to become the local expert, so I really marketed myself as the local expert not just in residential real estate, but in the town, in the history, in where you go to get a good pizza or where do you go to eat at a good restaurant on date night. Where can you find a good place to go for a hike around here?

The idea is that I can provide my clients with the most resourceful amount of information for this area, and by being the expert in one particular market, I can do that, and that allows me to be more useful to them rather than expanding myself beyond my reach. So, I do market myself as more of the local expert here in the Middletown area.

What's the biggest misconception/myth people have about working with a real estate agent?

I think for starters, one of the biggest myths that are out there is that as a buyer, when you go out there, you basically don't have to pay for a real estate agent. In Delaware, we are a free state with real estate agents on the buyer side, so when you call me to represent you as a buyer's agent, it's a free service to you. So, I think a big misconception for buyers is they're scared they might end up with added costs for them when they go shopping for a home.

One of my biggest specialties, and having said that my background is in new home constructions, I had spent six years with extensive training in new home construction and selling for them. I bring to the table a very big part of my expertise is what I know about new homes.

So for the buyer to go out, even in my area or any area, for that and to go purchase a new home, you could go into a builder's office and essentially the builder is represented by builder's rep and the builder's rep represents the builder, so essentially, they aren't representing you, so you walk in there unrepresented and you could have a realtor, specifically one who knows about new construction such as myself go with you and assist you in the process at no cost to you, and those who have that conception that they're going to walk in without a realtor and save money, that is a huge myth as well because the builders built into the overall financials, they already assumed that there is a realtor in the transaction and therefore there is that built into their bottom line. If you don't have a realtor, they're just going to get that extra profit and they leverage that over the total of their sales anyway as an average.

It's all more beneficial to you as a buyer to go in with a realtor, so you have that benefit of having a representative in there on your team representing you so that throughout the process you know that somebody is going to be looking out for your best interest because as much as you may like Jenny or Katie or whoever is in the sales office, that person is always going to default to whatever the new home builder tells them is the correct answer.

If I can tell anybody in this conversation to retain anything that I'm saying about a misconception of Realtors, it would be that, but you should always be represented when buying a new home because it doesn't cost you anything. It can only benefit you and you're not going to save any of their incentive money by not having one.

If you were to get a call from a family member in another state, wanting to sell their home, what advice would you give them about selecting an agent that can best serve their needs?

Well, obviously, we do have that amazing referral network, so yes, that would obviously be my first request is that they reach out to me so that I can connect them with a prescreened Keller Williams referral agent that I have talked to and tried to match based on their needs, but most importantly, when you're looking for an agent in your market and it's not in my market, I usually tell my family members or my friends, you have to look for somebody that is specifically in your zip code, somebody who knows your stats, somebody who has sold homes recently in your community or in your neighborhood or your school district or somewhere within a mile or two of your house with experience that has done it, somebody who has, I would say, like I said, statistics of how many days they've had on the market, percentage of list price and sales price, some clear statistics on their data so that you can look at that and really see that on paper.

Also, you're going to want to know what they're including with their listing service, what exactly is covered in their listing fees. Does it include professional photography? Does it include staging? Staging to me is a huge part of selling your home today. Every home should be staged professionally and it should be included in their listing service. I look for that in all of my friends and family's listing services. I think that's a huge deal.

How do they market their homes on social media? Social media is a big part of selling your home. Do they have a social media presence? If they're not on social media or they don't believe in social media, that's probably a red flag. How are they connected within your community? Do they have a big agent connection? Do they work with buyers? Do they only work with sellers?

There are a lot of these things that are going to have to weigh in before you'd make an agent decision. I definitely tell them, "Do not make a decision based on it being a friend or somebody that is saying, 'Hey, I'm a realtor, just give me a shot, I just signed up for school.'" This is a big financial decision. It's like playing with a quarter million dollars or half a million dollars out of your financial portfolio. Are you going to trust Aunt Susie with that kind of money just because she's your aunt? I think really what you have to think about is this is a big financial investment in your life, you have to be making this decision from strength and from intelligence and from data, so I would just really advise them to look carefully at the statistics.

How can someone that needs a real estate agent find out more about you and how you can help?

You can find me on my website at www.delawarelistings.com and on the website, you can click on the Email Me link or you can just call me, my phone number is right on there. There's also a link at the top of the website where there's a Facebook link, which will link you directly to my Facebook page, and my Facebook page is always full of staging tips, selling tips, buying tips and just general Middletown, Delaware information. You can always follow me on Facebook and private message me for anything that you might need, and I respond quickly. I look forward to anybody looking for any real estate information to reach out to me anytime.

About The Author

"Believe you can and you're halfway there." –Theodore Roosevelt

Keith is the #1 Best-Selling Author of Publish to Profit (Available on Amazon), Host of Business Innovators Radio and Real Estate Innovators Radio, Founder of Authority Surge, and an honored husband, father, and grandfather.

Keith has over 24 years of progressive experience in sales and marketing. As a lead generation expert, Keith strives to implement the most cost-effective automated sales systems to bring new business in a streamlined manner to sustain continued business growth.

He effectively develops and implements targeted action plans to maximize productivity, efficiency, and profitability.

He has an exceptional ability to research and evaluate industry trends and competitor products and use the findings when designing and executing innovative strategies to boost company leveraging.

To reach Keith you can contact him via email at keith.dougherty@gmail.com.

If you are a real estate professional, as in an agent, broker, broker associate, mortgage broker; a home inspector; an appraiser; a real estate lawyer; a title company; or any professional in real estate and you would like to apply to be on our show, you can apply at our website: RealEstateInnovatorsRadio.com

Please be patient as our guest list has grown significantly.

www.ingramcontent.com/pod-product-compliance
Lightning Source LLC
Chambersburg PA
CBHW071149200326
41519CB00018B/5172